Discover the world's best destinations with the Insight Guides Walking Eye app, available to download for free in the App Store and Google Play.

The container app provides easy access to fantastic free content on events and activities taking place in your current location or chosen destination, with the possibility of booking, as well as the regularly-updated Insight Guides travel blog: Inspire Me. In addition, you can purchase curated, premium destination guides through the app, which feature local highlights, hotel, bar, restaurant and shopping listings, an A to Z of practical information and more. Or purchase and download Insight Guides eBooks straight to your device.

TOP 10 ATTRACTIONS

TEGUISE
The former capital of Lanzarote is an attractive town that holds a busy market every Sunday. See page 45.

FUERTEVENTURA'S WINDMILLS
A reminder of a time before tourism. See page 63.

TIMANFAYA
An unforgettable volcanic landscape. See page 54.

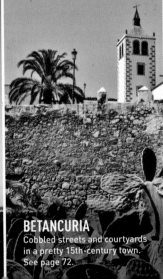

BETANCURIA
Cobbled streets and courtyards in a pretty 15th-century town. See page 72.

PÁJARA
A red sandstone doorway adorns the church in this picturesque village. See page 75.

COSTA CALMA
Sweeps of white sand draw visitors to Fuerteventura's Sotavento beaches. See page 78.

EL JABLE DUNES
These great empty swathes of sand lie just outside lively Corralejo in northern Fuerteventura. See page 68.

FUNDACIÓN CÉSAR MANRIQUE
The former home of Lanzarote's iconic artist and architect. See page 42.

CUEVA DE LOS VERDES
Take a trip through the dramatic lava-formed caves. See page 36.

PUERTO DEL CARMEN
Lanzarote's biggest resort offers some of the island's best beaches. See page 51.

A PERFECT TOUR

Day 1

Beach day
Spend the day exploring your base, Puerto del Carmen. Stroll along the attractive promenade, find a good spot to laze on Playa Grande, then enjoy a late fishy lunch at La Lonja (Calle Varadero).

Day 3

Arrecife and the Fundación Manrique
Visit the island capital, Arrecife, to explore the backstreets and have coffee by the Charco (lagoon). Then head to the Fundación César Manrique, a splendid museum and gallery in what was the artist's home, with murals, paintings, ceramics and views over the eerie volcanic landscape.

Day 4

Teguise
Head to Teguise when it is not market day (Sunday), so you can enjoy the pretty streets, admire the ornate colonial buildings and have lunch in the Ikarus Gastro Bar (Calle Clavijo y Fajardo). Just outside town, visit the hilltop Castillo de Santa Bárbara for stunning views and the fascinating Pirate Museum.

Day 2

The island interior
Drive through La Geria wine country, stopping at Bodega El Grifo to sample wine and explore the museum, then head towards the Monumento del Campesino in the centre of the island. Visit the adjoining artisan centre, then time your return journey to include an early (pre-booked) dinner (from 8pm) at the stunning La Tegala in Macher.

OF **LANZARETE**

Day 6

Mirador del Río and La Graciosa

Not far from Haría is the Parque Tropical, with exotic birds and subtropical plants. Continue to the far north of the island for lunch at the café at the Mirador del Río, from where there are spectacular views. You should have time for the short boat trip from nearby Orzola to La Graciosa, a completely undeveloped little island.

Day 8

Papagayo

Drive to Playa Blanca at the far south of the island. Stroll around this pretty resort and buy food for a picnic, then take a boat from the harbour for a 45-minute trip to the beautiful, and protected, Papagayo beaches.

Day 5

To the north

Book a night's accommodation in Haría, an arty little town in the verdant 'Valley of a Thousand Palms'. Go first to the extraordinary underground world of the Jameos del Agua (another Manrique creation) then return to Haría for a late lunch at Dos Hermanos (Plaza León y Castillo).

Day 7

Parque Nacional de Timanfaya

Back at Puerto del Carmen, drive via the idyllic village of Yaiza to the Parque Nacional de Timanfaya. Go for a camel ride at the Echado de Camellos then take a tour around the Montañas del Fuego, before eating meat grilled over natural volcanic heat at El Diablo restaurant.

CONTENTS

INTRODUCTION

Swept by trade winds and warmed by coastal currents, the islands of Lanzarote and Fuerteventura offer a consistently warm climate, with some 300 days of sunshine a year. They are part of the Canary Islands, which lie approximately 1,100km (690 miles) southwest of the Spanish mainland and, at the nearest point, 115km (70 miles) from the West African coast. Although part of Spain, in 1982 the islands became an autonomous province, divided in two: the eastern islands, which include Lanzarote and Fuerteventura, are governed by a Cabildo Insular (Island Council) from Las Palmas de Gran Canaria, the western islands from Santa Cruz de Tenerife.

Lanzarote is some 60km (38 miles) in length and 24km (15 miles) across at its widest point, with a population of about 145,000, of whom some 58,000 live in the capital, Arrecife. Fuerteventura is larger, at around 100km (60 miles) long and 30km (18 miles) wide, but sparsely populated – there are around 115,000 inhabitants, of whom about half live in Puerto del Rosario.

LANDSCAPE AND CLIMATE

The whole volcanic archipelago is barren, but Lanzarote and Fuerteventura are drier and more barren than the rest. Lanzarote's last volcanic explosion was in 1824, but the heat is still close to the surface, as you will find if you go to the Parque Nacional Timanfaya, and much of the island is still covered with cindery *malpaís* (badlands). Fuerteventura has seen no volcanic activity for some 5,000 years, but has less rain than any of the islands, and the landscape is coloured in shades of brown and khaki, with great expanses of dunes.

Lanzarote's highest point is Montaña Blanca, at 670m (2,198ft). The beaches around the major resorts, especially the famous ones at Puerto del Carmen, are covered with golden sands, as are the beautiful stretches close to Playa Blanca, while smaller, rockier coves retain their black volcanic sand. Of Fuerteventura's 152 beaches, some 50km (32 miles) consist of white sand, while about 25km (15 miles) are black volcanic shingle. The highest point on the island is Monte Jandía (807m/2,648ft).

Playa Blanca, a beach at the resort with the same name

The islands' average annual temperature is 20°C (68°F), soaring in high summer to 28–30°C (82–86°F). Fuerteventura is usually windy – one explanation for the island's name is that it comes from *viento fuerte* (strong wind). On both islands, early mornings can be cloudy before blue skies and sunshine take over. There is little rain – what there is falls mostly between October and January. In summer the islands sometimes suffer from what is known as *tiempo Africano* (African weather), when the hot sirocco wind sweeps up from the Sahara, covering the landscape with reddish dust.

VEGETATION AND FARMING

There are few trees, apart fom the Canary palms (*Phoenix Canariensis*) in the Haría Valley, and those planted along the roadsides of many towns and resorts. Parks, hotel grounds and botanical gardens are bright with exotic plants brought to the island from southern Africa, South America and elsewhere that flourish happily in the islands' subtropical climate. The Strelitzia (bird-of-paradise flower) is one of the most showy, but hibiscus, poinsettia and agave are also common, and vividly coloured bougainvillea rampages over the garden walls and facades of villas and hotels.

Various forms of *Euphorbia* (spurge) flourish on the scrubby soil, including the *Euphorbia Canariensis* (candelabra spurge) and the rare, cactus-like *cardón de Jandía* (*Euphorbia handiensis*), found in the south of Fuerteventura.

A variety of prickly pear cactus cultivated mainly on Lanzarote is the nopal, on which the cochineal beetle feeds. When crushed, the beetle produces a red dye – cochineal. This is not the lucrative industry it was in the 19th century (see page 19), but a recent resurgence of interest in natural products means cochineal is being produced in Lanzarote, but on a much smaller scale.

Another form of vegetation is that produced on the black lava called *picón*. This cinder, which collects and stores moisture from dew, is spread over arid soil and used for the cultivation of vines – especially in the La Geria region.

Aloe vera

On both islands you will see aloe vera, another cactus-like plant that has become very popular for medicinal and cosmetic purposes – especially to soothe sunburn – and is being widely cultivated. The plant has long, greyish-green spiky leaves and spears of yellow flowers. You will find the products for sale in small shops, markets and supermarkets all over the islands.

WILDLIFE

There is plenty for bird-watchers to spot on both islands in winter. Lanzarote's central plain is the best place to see Houbara bustards, kestrels, stone curlews and trumpeter finches – which are also found on Fuerteventura, along with the Fuerteventura chat. Berthelot's pipit can be seen all over the island, hoopoes are fairly common, and chiffchaffs and warblers are often found in urban settings. The Salinas de Janubio (salt pans) are a stopping-off place for many migratory birds, and numerous seabirds cluster on the offshore islands.

Traditional costumes and music at a Lanzarote fiesta

There are few mammals on either island: bats, rats, mice, squirrels, rabbits and hedgehogs are about the sum of it. There are reptiles, though: geckos and lizards. The water around the islands is home to dolphins, porpoises and whales, and is rich in fish, including *corvina* (a kind of sea bass), *cherne* (wreckfish or stone bass), *sama* (sea bream) and *vieja* (parrot fish), as well as more homely *sardinas* (sardines).

PEOPLE AND LANGUAGE

The people of the Canary Islands have a strong sense of their identity as islanders and are keen to stress that they are *canarios* first and foremost. Spanish (*castellano*) is the language of the islands, but there are subtle differences from the peninsula, many of which reflect the two-way traffic between the Canaries and Latin America. Final consonants are swallowed and 'z' is pronounced 's', as in the Americas, rather than the lisped 'th' of mainland Spain. A number of Latino words have been borrowed, too: a bus is a *guagua* and potatoes are *papas*.

The resort of Caleta de Fuste on Fuerteventura

TOURISM

Traditionally, the islands' economy has been dependent on agriculture, but the principal source of revenue today is tourism. The strong winds and good waves attract surfing enthusiasts, but, apart from this, the equable climate means that the islands are all-round holiday destinations, with many older northern European visitors favouring the cooler months as an escape from their own harsher winters, while families are in the majority during school holidays. That Lanzarote has escaped the high-rise desecration that has spoiled parts of Tenerife and Gran Canaria is due in large part to the artist César Manrique (see page 27), who was influential in persuading the authorities to work with the island's landscape and natural features. Fuerteventura has some rather characterless resorts, but on the whole they are not badly done.

From volcanic landscapes to sandy beaches, the islands have much to offer, whether visitors are looking for water sports or family entertainment, or are keen to discover the island way of life. The islands are easy to get around on well-surfaced roads, and there are some pleasant walking routes. *Turismo rural* has gained a foothold, making it possible to stay in rural properties in beautiful surroundings (see page 135) and sample traditional food. All in all, enough to convince most people that the islands merit one of their early names – the Fortunate Isles.

A BRIEF HISTORY

The Canary Islands have been part of Spain since they were con-
quered in the late 15th century, but there was a flourishing culture here long before that, although no one is quite sure where
the pre-Hispanic people came from. These early inhabitants are
known collectively as the Guanches, although strictly speaking
this was the name of a tribe that inhabited Tenerife. The people of
Lanzarote and Fuerteventura prefer the name Majoreros, which
is derived from Fuerteventura's indigenous name – Maxorata.
Some historians think the original inhabitants were related to
the Canarii people, who lived on the Saharan side of the Atlas
Mountains. But as far as we know, the Guanches had no boats,
so how they crossed from the African coast remains a mystery.

The Guanches (or Majo-
reros) were an agricultural
people who mostly lived
in groups of caves, but on
the three eastern islands
they also built houses. On
Lanzarote and Fuerteventura
their dwellings were grouped
into hamlets around the
edges of lava fields. Their
society had a hierarchi-
cal structure, with kings –
guanartemes – and priests
– *faycans*. Lanzarote was
a single kingdom, but on
Fuerteventura there were
two – Maxorata in the north

Marital custom

Scientist and explorer Alex-
ander von Humboldt, who
visited Lanzarote in 1799
en route to South America,
claimed the indigenous people had an unusual custom:
'A woman had several hus-
bands, who each took it in
turn to exercise the rights of
the head of the family. Each
husband was known as such
during a lunar month; then
another took his place while
he returned to being a serv-
ant in the house.'

and Jandía in the south, beyond La Pared, the wall that once stretched across the narrowest part of the island. These early people mummified their dead and buried them in caves or stone-lined graves, and it is evidence from mummies that has led scientists to place the islanders' ethnic origins in northwest Africa.

The Guanches did not have the wheel, they knew nothing of metalworking and did not use bows and arrows – their main weapons were wooden spears. Domestic implements were made from stone and bone or from obsidian, a black, volcanic glass. Porous lava was made into millstones and mortars. Their vessels and containers were made from pottery, wood, leather and woven cane. *Gofio*, toasted flour originally made from barley, was their staple food, but they also ate a variety of roots, wild fruits and berries. Pigs, sheep and goats provided meat as well as the materials for shelters, containers and clothes, and milk also came from sheep and goats. Fish formed a part of their diet, even when they had to travel some distance down to the coast to find it.

ARRIVAL OF THE EUROPEANS

The first documented account of a European expedition to the Canary Islands was in 1339, when the Genoese Lanzarotto Malocello discovered the island that was named after him. The first detailed description of the islands was written two years later by Genoese historian Nicoloso da Recco, who accompanied a slave-traders' voyage. He wrote: 'The natives of Fuerteventura are few in number and live on meat and milk, and are of great stature, and are very firm in their beliefs.' Various expeditions were mounted during the course of the century, but it was not until 1402 that the first conquerors arrived. Jean de Béthencourt and Gadifer de la Salle, Norman noblemen who had pledged allegiance to the king of Castile, claimed Lanzarote, Fuerteventura and El Hierro for their royal master, but failed to take Gran Canaria and Tenerife. Like most conquerors, they claimed the expedition was 'for the exaltation of the Christian faith', so they must have been delighted when the last king of Lanzarote, after several failed escape attempts, agreed to Christian baptism.

Jean de Béthencourt

Many of the indigenous people were sold into slavery and many more died of European diseases, but those who survived intermarried with the colonisers, who settled down to a harsh life, making their living from the land and sea.

It was not until 1478 that another attempt was made to conquer the two larger islands, under the aegis of Ferdinand and Isabella – the so-called Catholic Monarchs of a newly united Spain. It took several years to subdue the indigenous people, but eventually all the Canary Islands became Spanish possessions.

Because of their location, the islands were vital for Spanish colonisation in the Americas. This revolved around slavery and sugar cane, both of which were introduced to the Americas from the Canaries, but it was Gran Canaria and Tenerife that were the main beneficiaries. Of no interest to their Spanish masters and with little source of income, many inhabitants of Lanzarote and Fuerteventura turned to piracy during the 16th and early 17th centuries, a somewhat precarious way of earning a living, and one that laid them open to reciprocal attacks.

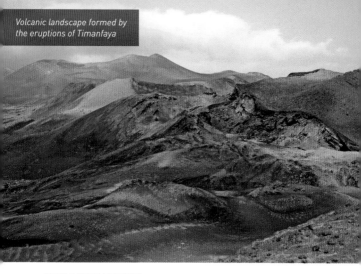
Volcanic landscape formed by the eruptions of Timanfaya

EXPLOSIVE EVENTS

During the mid-18th century, memories of pirate raids faded into insignificance when Lanzarote experienced a disastrous series of volcanic eruptions. In 1730, Volcán Timanfaya erupted, and continued to pour molten lava and black ash down its slopes for a further six years, until a third of the island had been devastated, many of its inhabitants had fled to Gran Canaria and some had set out on the long journey to Latin America. For almost a century the volcano appeared to sleep, but 1824 saw another series of eruptions, albeit smaller ones. Visitors to the dark, eerie landscape now protected as the Parque Nacional de Timanfaya may be able to visualise the devastation.

Although the eruptions overwhelmed the most fertile part of the island, the volcanic ash formed *picón*, dark cinders that collect and retain the dew, forming a natural irrigation system. On this the islanders were able to grow a variety of vegetables, and to profit from the cultivation of vines and the export of wine, ushering in a period of prosperity that lasted until the early years of the 19th century. This system, known as *enarenad*, was later practised in arid parts of the Spanish mainland, although silicon sand was used instead of cinder.

The next money-spinner was cochineal, a red dye created by crushing the beetle *(Dactylopius coccus costa)* that fed on the nopal cactus, and which was introduced to the islands in around 1825. For some 50 years the industry flourished, before the creation of aniline dyes made it largely superfluous.

During the latter part of this period the larger, more powerful islands of Gran Canaria and Tenerife were flexing their muscles, demanding a degree of independence from Spain and vying with each other for supremacy at the same time. Tenerife, which had profited from the wine trade (Gran Canaria's soil was unsuitable for viniculture) and other long-distance commerce was by far the wealthier and had established a university in the town of La Laguna, which became an intellectual centre. Gran Canaria resented Tenerife's powerful position and, under the late 19th-century leadership of Fernando León y Castillo, foreign minister in the national government, made a bid for supremacy.

In 1903, emboldened by Cuba gaining freedom from Spain five years earlier, the Partido Local Canario was formed, with the aim of achieving some degree of

Mountain of fire

The parish priest of Yaiza, Andrés Lorenzo Curbelo, described the 1730 eruption as 'an enormous mountain that rose out of the bosom of the earth. From its flat top flames belched out and continued burning for 19 days'. Several months later 'new eruptions came... [with] incandescent streams of lava, together with the densest smoke'.

independence and dividing the archipelago into two provinces. This was formalised in 1927, but brought little economic relief to the islands, whose trade had been badly hit by World War I and its economic aftermath. Lanzarote and Fuerteventura became part of the Eastern Province, governed, as they are today, from Las Palmas de Gran Canaria. The seat of island government (Cabildo Insular) alternates between Las Palmas and Santa Cruz de Tenerife every four years.

There had been a steady flow of people from the Canaries to the Americas since the late 16th century, but agricultural decline in the late 19th and early 20th centuries increased this traffic, as people went looking for a better way of life. Remittances were sent home, and many of those who made good returned to the islands and built homes or established small businesses, thus accentuating the ties with Latin America that are still apparent today.

POLITICAL UPHEAVALS

In 1924, under the dictatorship of Miguel Primo de Rivera, Fuerteventura, the bleakest of the Canary Islands, was judged a suitable place to send political dissidents. Writer and philosopher Miguel de Unamuno was the best known of these. He came to love the island, which he described as 'a rock thirsting in the sun, a treasure of health and honesty'. There is a monument to him in the north of the island.

Praise from Castro

Fidel Castro expressed his admiration for Canarian emigrants to Cuba, who 'helped forge the country with their proverbial hard work'. It was from them, he said, that 'our peasants inherited their seriousness, their decency, their sense of honour and also their rebelliousness'.

Franciso Franco and his officers, 1936

In 1936, the three-year Spanish Civil War began, initiated by Francisco Franco, military governor of the Canary Islands. He spent the last night before launching his coup in the Hotel Madrid in Las Palmas.

After the bitter Civil War and World War II, the Canaries, like the rest of Spain, initially suffered from political isolation and economic hardship. Things improved a little in the 1950s, when Spain was once more recognised by the international community, but it was the advent of tourism in the following decade that really turned the tide.

Franco remained in power until his death in 1975, when his authoritarian regime was replaced by democratic government. The new Spanish Constitution of 1978 created the Autonomous Region of the Canary Islands – now one of 17 such regions. The archipelago is not completely separate from Spain, but the island government, the Cabildo Insular, does have a great deal of freedom.

Grape harvest, Bodega La Geria, Lanzarote

In the national elections of 1996, the Coalición Canaria, a union of regional parties, took four seats in the Madrid parliament (reduced to three in 2004, two in 2008/2011 and just one in 2016). It now sees its role as working with the national government to win improvements for the islands, rather than looking for further independence. This is not to say that no resentment is felt towards Madrid, but resentment of central government is, perhaps, a fact of life wherever regional feelings are strong.

Many mainland Spaniards, particularly from the poorer regions – Andalusia and Galicia – are to be found working in the islands' service industries. They have integrated well into island life and, while there is some dissatisfaction expressed about them doing jobs that might be done by local people, there is relatively little ill-feeling.

The islands have enjoyed considerable commercial freedom and tax exemptions ever since the 19th century. When Spain became a full member of the European Union, fiscal changes had to be introduced, but important tax privileges were negotiated. Motorists will be pleased to find that, in a period of rocketing fuel prices, the islands still have the cheapest petrol in Europe.

TOURISM, ECONOMY AND ENVIRONMENT

Traditionally, the economy of the islands has been dependent on agriculture and fishing, but the principal source of employment and revenue today is in the service sector, of which tourism is a major part. Some 90 percent of Lanzarote's inhabitants work in the tourist industry and the infrastructure that supports it, and the percentage in Fuerteventura is similar. When Arrecife airport opened in the early 1960s, tourism started to take off. Fuerteventura's airport opened in 1969, and while the growth of the tourist industry was slower here than on the other islands, it has exploded in recent years. Lanzarote now receives about 3 million visitors annually,

⊘ DANGEROUS JOURNEYS

Lanzarote and Fuerteventura have become the main route into Europe for illegal immigrants from Africa now that strict controls have made it more difficult for them to cross from northern Morocco to southern Spain. Desperate people, many from war-torn sub-Saharan regions, pay traffickers up to €1,200 (around £1,000) to reach the Moroccan coast, where they are loaded onboard small, ill-equipped boats to make the dangerous journey to these islands, which are the closest to the African coast. Many drown, or die of dehydration, during the course of their journey. Others reach the island shores to face an uncertain future.

Turbines utilise the strong winds the islands receive

Fuerteventura 3.2 million, mainly English, Germans and Scandinavians. There are believed to be more than 50,000 foreign property owners on Lanzarote, and some have established bars, clubs and other small businesses. There are fewer homeowners on Fuerteventura, but numbers are rising.

The eastern islands suffer from severe water shortage (they receive less rainfall than parts of the Sahara), a problem intensified by the strain that so many visitors place on the system. The creation of desalination plants has helped, but visitors should try to be frugal in their use of water, although in hot summer weather it can be rather difficult.

The availability of work in the tourist industry has encouraged many young people to desert the land and the fishing industry (although Arrecife still has the biggest fishing fleet in the Canaries) in favour of higher wages and more fun in the resorts. But life for the islanders has rarely been easy, and it is understandable that the latest generation should look for alternatives. Most people believe that tourism has brought more advantages than disadvantages to the islands, and that the inhabitants' individuality and love of their lands will enable them to retain their special character, despite the many changes.

HISTORICAL LANDMARKS

c.2nd–1st centuries BC Settlements of Guanches in Canary Islands.

AD1339 Genoese Lanzarotto Malocello discovers Lanzarote.

1402 Jean de Béthencourt and Gadifer de la Salle invade and claim Lanzarote, Fuerteventura and El Hierro.

1478–83 Canary Islands brought under control of Spanish Crown.

16th–17th centuries Many inhabitants of impoverished Lanzarote and Fuerteventura turn to piracy.

1730–6 Continuous eruptions of Mount Timanfaya; a third of Lanzarote is devastated.

1730–1950 Poverty forces widespread emigration to Latin America.

1825–75 Economic boom follows the introduction of the cochineal beetle, but the industry is ruined by the invention of aniline dyes.

1852 Isabella II declares the Canary Islands a Free Trade Zone.

1911 Self-administration council – Cabildo Insular – introduced.

1927 Canary Islands are divided in two. Lanzarote and Fuerteventura become part of the Eastern Province, governed from Gran Canaria.

1936 Franco initiates the three-year Spanish Civil War.

1962 Lanzarote's Arrecife airport opens. Tourism rapidly develops into the most important industry.

1969 Fuerteventura airport opens. Tourism develops more slowly here.

1970s Influenced by artist and architect César Manrique, the Cabildo imposes strict building regulations on Lanzarote.

1978–82 Spanish Constitution joins the two island provinces to form the Autonomous Region of the Canary Islands.

1995 Islands integrated into the EU but retain important tax privileges.

2002 The euro becomes the national currency.

2014 After 14 years and countless protests, the Spanish petrol giant Repsol finally abandons oil explorations off the coast.

2015 The nationalist Coalición Canaria (CC) wins elections in Lanzarote closely followed by the socialist PSOE and the left-wing Podemos party.

2017 Lanzarote's Jardín de Cactus (Cactus Garden) is awarded the prestigious International Carlo Scarpa Prize for Gardens.

One of Playa Blanca's inviting beaches

WHERE TO GO

LANZAROTE

Lanzarote is a small island, but it packs a lot of contrasts into a limited space. From the awesome, unearthly Montañas del Fuego in the Parque Nacional de Timanfaya to the verdant 'Valley of a Thousand Palms' around Haría; from the tranquillity of La Graciosa to the razzmatazz of Puerto del Carmen, there is always something to surprise the visitor. One thing is consistent, however: the building limits proposed by artist César Manrique and imposed by the island government have ensured that, with a few exceptions, the architecture consists of low white buildings with green, blue or brown balconies and shutters, which complement the indigenous architecture of the island.

Lanzarote is an easy place to get around. For the sake of simplicity this guide starts with the capital, Arrecife, then divides the island into three areas: north, south and centre. However, distances are so small that you may find yourself straying from one region to the other on a single trip. Just follow your own instincts and you won't go far wrong.

ARRECIFE

Arrecife ❶ lies 8km (5 miles) east of the airport, from where it is well served by inexpensive taxis. Buses *(guaguas)* run every 20 minutes to Costa Teguise and Puerto del Carmen, and taxi fares to both resorts are very reasonable. The town has a long history, as its two sturdy fortresses demonstrate. Castillo de San Gabriel was built in the second half of the 17th century to reinforce the town against attacks from the sea; it was the work of Genoese engineer Leonardo Torriani, who also built Teguise's Castillo de

Santa Bárbara. The Castillo de San José dates from about a century later, when pirate attacks were still a problem. It was also a work-creation project, as the islanders were suffering great poverty following periods of drought and the eruption of Timanfaya, which had destroyed farmland in the most fertile part of the island. For a long time it was known as the Castillo del Hambre (Fortress of Hunger). In 1852, when links with Spain's American colonies meant that it made more sense to have a capital on the coast, Arrecife took over from Teguise as the capital of Lanzarote.

Arrecife is a down-to-earth, working city, home to almost half the island's population. It has few buildings of architectural interest and not a great deal in the way of culture, but it is well worth a visit to see a slice of island life, away from the resorts or the picture-postcard villages. It has a few decent tapas bars,

Quiosco de la Música

an excellent restaurant in the Castillo de San José, food to be purchased in the market and local shops that is cheaper and more varied than in the resorts, and an excellent curved beach – Playa Reducto – with golden sands and calm, safe waters. If you want a quiet holiday there is a lot to be said for making a base here in one of the seafront hotels.

Exploring the Town

If you come to Arrecife by car, get off the *circunvalación* (ring road) at the west (airport) end of town, where you can park in a large car park at the end of the beach, opposite the smart Cabildo Insular building, and thereby avoid the narrow streets and one-way system of the city. Looming at the other end of the beach is the 17-storey **Arrecife Gran Hotel & Spa**. This was the building that so upset Manrique when he returned from New York that he took steps to ensure that Lanzarote's skyline would not become disfigured by similar high-rises. Although it breaks all the rules, it is a sleek, well-designed building. Take the glass lift to the top, where a there's a restaurant and a café that offers views over the town and down to Puerto del Carmen.

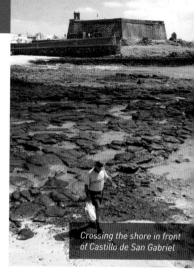

Crossing the shore in front of Castillo de San Gabriel

Newly planted gardens and a wooden walkway lead towards the town centre. On a corner, opposite an attractive Canarian-style building belonging to the Cabildo, old men sit in a little square playing dominoes. A broad promenade runs east from here. The statue at the beginning is of Blas Cabrera Felipe (1878–1945), an eminent scientist who was born in the town. There are seats in flower-decked bowers, and egrets squawk and flap in the palm trees. The circular wooden **Quiosco de la Música**, where a band sometimes plays, also serves as the town's tourist information office. On the other side of the road, the Avenida de la Marina, is the post office and the **Casa de Cultura Agustín de la Hoz Ⓐ**, which contains early murals by César Manrique discovered during the course of renovation.

Cross a little bridge to the **Castillo de San Gabriel B**, with a rusty cannon standing outside. The sturdy little fortress now houses the **Museo de Historia de Arrecife** (Mon–Fri 10am–5pm, Sat 10am–2pm), with information about the Guanches (or Majoreros), the island's original inhabitants, its fauna, flora and history. You can cross back to the seafront via a parallel bridge, the **Puente de las Bolas**, named for the cannon balls atop its twin pillars. Follow the promenade (now called Avenida Coll) a short way to the right (towards the port), passing the Ayuntamiento (Town Hall), then cross the road to the **Charco de San Ginés C**. This pretty little tidal lagoon, where boats bob serenely on the water, is surrounded by brightly shuttered buildings, several of which house restaurants. There is a traditional fair held every Wed and Thu. The only incongruous

⊙ LEÓN Y CASTILLO

You may wonder why most towns and villages in Lanzarote have a street or square called León y Castillo. This has nothing to do with lions or castles, but pays homage to two brothers, Fernando and Juan, who were born in Telde, Gran Canaria, where there is now a museum devoted to them. Fernando, who became foreign minister in the Spanish government in 1881, implemented a programme of improvements to the port of Las Palmas, the plans for which were drawn up by his engineer brother Juan. This made it the major port in the archipelago and an important stop on the new steamship route to the West Indies, and changed the ailing fortunes of Gran Canaria and, by extension, of Lanzarote and Fuerteventura.

Charco de San Ginés

feature is a large, four-screen cinema (Multicines Atlántida) but local people are probably glad of the entertainment.

You can walk all the way round the lagoon then off into the town to the Plaza de las Palmas, and the parish church, the **Iglesia de San Ginés Obispo** (daily 9am–1pm, 5–7pm), with a distinctive white cupola topping its bell tower. It is dedicated to the town's patron saint, whose festival is celebrated here in August. There is a simple interior, with a good Mudéjar ceiling of dark wood. If you find the church closed, just sit on one of the benches in the shady square, listen to the drip of a central fountain and admire the exterior of the building.

Narrow lanes lead from the square into the centre of the town, focused on the pedestrianised shopping street, **Calle León y Castillo**, running back from the seafront. Here, branches of well-known stores such as Zara and Mango share space with the large HiperDino supermarket and a

Castillo de San José

few delightfully old-fashioned shops.

Art in Arrecife

Go west, via the oblong Plaza de la Constitución towards Calle Betancort. Here (No. 33) you will find **El Almacén** , a cultural centre (Mon–Sat 10am–11.45pm) in an old store converted by César Manrique. The centre includes two galleries and, on the top floor, the Cine Buñuel, which screens art house films.

Arrecife is a small town, and all of the above can easily be done on foot, but to visit the last place of interest you need to take a taxi. They are readily available, and it should cost no more than €5 from the centre to the **Castillo de San José** **E**, which houses the **Museo Internacional de Arte Contemporáneo** (MIAC; www.cactlanzarote.com; daily 10am–8pm). The fortress had fallen into disrepair by the 20th century, and in 1975 Manrique directed the renovation of the building and founded the Museum of Contemporary Art. In a series of cool rooms within the thick stone walls is a collection of paintings, sketches and sculpture by internationally known artists such as Antoni Tàpies, as well as Manrique himself and other renowned Canarian artists.

Down a flight of stairs more paintings decorate the walls of the **QuéMUAC** restaurant and coffee shop (restaurant Tue–Sat noon–4pm, Fri–Sat also 7–11pm; coffee shop daily 10am–1pm; cocktail bar Fri–Sat 10pm–1am). From the floor-to-ceiling windows there is a view of the new Puerto de los Mármoles – not traditionally picturesque, but in this context the cranes, ships and containers have a sculptural beauty. You can eat very well, very reasonably here (see page 115), or just enjoy the view from a low, comfy bar stool while you have a drink.

THE NORTH

The north of the island is a treasure trove of natural wonders and man-made attractions. Nature has given us the dramatic cliffs of Risco de Famara on the west coast, the *malpaís* (badlands) on the east, the fascinating Cueva de los Verdes and the tranquil island of Isla La Graciosa, while man (or, to be specific, Manrique) has created the breathtaking Jameos del Agua, the Jardín de Cactus and the Mirador del Río.

Jardín de Cactus and Arrieta

From the *circunvalación* around Arrecife, take the LZ1 north towards **Guatiza** to visit the **Jardín de Cactus** ❷ (www.cactlanzarote. com; daily 10am–5.45pm, July–Sept 9am–5.45pm). As you enter Guatiza you pass fields of cultivated cactus, for this is the region where cochineal is still produced (see page 19). Set in a volcanic crater, this Manrique-designed garden spirals in a circle of terraces up to a small windmill. There are

Jardín de Cactus

cacti of all kinds: round and dumpy, tall and phallic, and some like little furry creatures snuggled in the volcanic soil. The garden boasts around 450 different species from five continents. Manrique's designs on the external walls of the toilets are attractions in themselves. This was the artist's last gift for his beloved island. In 2017, Manrique's masterpiece was awarded the prestigious International Carlo Scarpa Prize for Gardens.

En route from Guatiza to the Jameos del Agua, you could make a brief detour to **Arrieta ❸**. We are in Manrique country here, and one of his sculptures, like a giant wind chime, stands at a roundabout where a road leads the short distance to this tiny fishing village. To the right, before you enter the village, you could turn off to the pleasant **Playa de la Garita**. Arrieta is a sleepy place, although popular with divers, and it gets animated at weekend lunch times when several fish restaurants around the small harbour draw customers. Also worth a visit is the Aloe Vera House (www.aloepluslanzarote.es; Calle Cortijo 2; Mon–Sat 10am–6pm; free), which has lots of information on the production and uses of the plant.

A sad tale

A strange house stands on one of Arrieta's jetties, pagoda-like in bright blue and brick-red. The building has a sad story to tell: in the 1920s a local man emigrated to Argentina, where he prospered, but when his young daughter fell gravely ill, he was advised that the Atlantic winds would be good for her. He returned to Arrieta and built a house as exposed to the elements as possible, in a style popular in Argentina. Sadly, the daughter died, despite his care, and is buried in the local cemetery.

Jameos del Agua and Cueva de los Verdes

Continue north for 3km (2 miles) to the well-signposted **Jameos del Agua ❹** (www.

At the Jameos del Agua

cactlanzarote.com; daily 10am–6.30pm, Tue and Sat (and Wed in summer) until 12.30am). You turn off onto a road that is in many places not wide enough for two-way traffic, but there are many passing places, and people are usually courteous about using them. This is one site that just about everybody comes to, so it can get busy – try to come fairly early, or at the end of the day – and it is like nothing else you will ever have seen. It is part of a volcanic tunnel system that runs from Montaña de Corona, which erupted about 4,000 years ago, out into the Atlantic. It was this eruption that created the *malpaís* (now a protected area) through which you will drive if you continue north. A *jameo* is the name for a cavity produced when the roof of a volcanic tunnel collapses.

Within this one, Manrique created an extraordinary underground world. You go down steps to the *jameo chico* (small cave) to a bar/restaurant (bar daily 10am–6.30pm, restaurant daily noon–4pm, Tue and Sat (and Wed in summer) also 7–11pm), full of lush foliage and soft music, from where narrow paths lead to a saltwater lake of varying depth depending on the tide. The lake is home to a unique variety of crab *(Munidopsis polymorpha)*, white, blind and without shells – as they have no predators, they had no need to develop them. Notices around the lake tell you that it is forbidden to throw coins into the water, as their corrosion would endanger the crabs. At the other side of the lake, landscaped terraces lead up to ground level. At the far side is a 550-seat auditorium, with splendid acoustics. A museum here, the **Casa de los Volcanes** (Mon–Fri 10am–6.30pm) is a volcanology study centre.

About 1km (0.8 miles) up a narrow road opposite lies the **Cueva de los Verdes ⑤** (www.cactlanzarote.com; daily 10am–6pm, in summer until 7pm, guided tour). *Verde* means green, but the name refers not to the colour of the rocks but to a fam-

ily called Verde who used to keep goats in the upper part of the cave. Over the years, these caverns served as a place of refuge for local people when pirates attacked. The cave system is part of the same 'tube' that runs from Montaña de Corona to the sea.

You may have to wait a short while to go in as the numbers on each 50-minute tour are limited; however, they run very frequently. The temperature inside the caves remains at 18–20°C (64–68°F)

Cueva de los Verdes

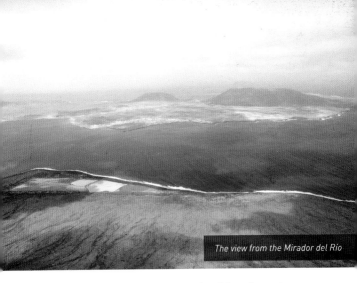

The view from the Mirador del Río

throughout the year, which makes the visit a pleasant escape from summer heat. Claustrophobics should be fine though, as, after an initial low, narrow stretch, the cave opens out into a vast cavern, and thereafter there are few places where you need to stoop. The tour does involve shuffling along rather slowly but it's worth it, as the shapes of the cave walls and ceilings, formed by the solidified lava and enhanced by discreet lighting, are extraordinary. Your guide will lead you into an auditorium, where concerts are sometimes held, as the acoustics are excellent. As the tour draws to an end, the guide will demand silence in order to introduce you to the rather ingenious 'secret of the caves'.

Mirador del Río and Parque Tropical

Continue north, through cindery *malpaís*, where only lichen-covered rocks and euphorbia bushes enliven the black terrain. After a while a few small vineyards appear, the vines planted in the traditional Lanzarote way, within a semicircle of rocks (see page 50). On a hillside, a bodega offers tastings and sells wine. The road ends at the **Mirador del Río** (www.cactlanzarote.com; daily 10am–5.45pm, in summer until 6.45pm). You will not be surprised to learn that it was Manrique who transformed this disused gun emplacement into a lookout point and glass-fronted café. The views are stupendous, encompassing La Graciosa, with the smaller islands of Montaña Clara and Alegranza in the distance. The stretch of water separating Graciosa from the mainland is called *El Río* (river) but is, in fact, a narrow channel in the Atlantic.

A clifftop stretch of road leads along the Risco de Famara, then to lower ground. The views are wonderful, but don't stop to enjoy them until you find a suitable place, as the road is very narrow.

Haría

Continuing south, you drop down into the greenest, most fertile part of the island, the valley of **Haría ❻**, known as the 'Valley of a Thousand Palms'. This is an exaggeration, but there are quite a lot of them. As tour guides and brochures are keen to point out, the legend recounts that once upon a time a palm tree was planted for every girl born locally, and two for every boy. Haría is a nice little town. Spick and span in white and green, it has

attracted a number of artists and artisans in its time, and became Manrique's home during his later years. The **Casa-Museo César Manrique** (www.fcmanrique.org; daily 10.30am–6pm) is a beautifully decorated house, full of personal belongings

Parking in Orzola

There are car parks just inland from Orzola harbour; the bays directly in front of it only allow you to park for 2.5 hours – no good if you're going to the island.

and tools, with two patios and a separate workshop, that hasn't changed from the day the artist died. The church, **Nuestra Señora de la Encarnación**, is a modern copy of the 17th-century original which was damaged by a storm, then destroyed, in the 1950s. There's a good **craft market** in the square around the church (Plaza de León y Castillo) every Saturday (10am–2.30pm). Much of the work on sale is made at

Daredevil goat at Las Pardelas

the **Taller de Artesanía** (Tue–Sat 10am–1.30pm, 4–7pm, Mon 10am–1.30pm; free), a craft-workers' co-operative.

Orzola and La Graciosa

At the tip of the island, with its back to the badlands, lies the village of **Orzola**, jumping-off point for La Graciosa. There's not much to Orzola, apart from a number of good fish restaurants (see page 116), from the terraces of which you can watch the comings and goings of boats to the island (see page 85). The trip to **La Graciosa** ❼ takes about 20 minutes, but it leads you into another world. Part of the protected **Parque Natural del Archipélago Chinijo**, it has only one settlement, Caleta del Sebo, and a population of 700. There are no cars, except a few Land Rovers and, apart from the *paseo* around the harbour, no paved roads. To get around, you have to walk, or hire a bike, which is easily done from a couple of outlets by the port. There are several fish restaurants around the harbour and in the streets behind it, but if you come on a weekday they may not all be open. Most people buy picnic supplies from one of three little supermarkets and head for the beaches. There's a small golden beach and protected waters right by the harbour where local children splash about, but the better beaches are a little way away. The currents are very strong, so swimming is not a good idea. Paddle instead, and explore the rock pools where tiny fish swim around your feet.

If you are back at the harbour around 3pm you'll see the fishing smacks come in, and you can watch as small fish are unloaded from the decks into wheelbarrows and taken a few yards away to be laid out on the jetty to dry in the sun. These are *pejines*; when dried, they are grilled and eaten as tapas.

Back on the mainland, going south from Orzola, the best route is along the coast, but there is a narrow lane out of the village that takes you back to the main Arrieta to Mirador del Río road, and a short way up the lane is **Las Pardelas ❽** (www.pardelas-park.com; daily 10am–6pm, until 7pm in spring and summer). This friendly, family-run ecological park with indigenous plants, domestic animals and donkey rides has a small restaurant, and makes a nice gentle stop if you are travelling with children.

THE CENTRE

The centre of the island is where you will find the airport, the capital, Arrecife, the two largest resorts, Puerto del Carmen and Costa de Teguise, the historic town of Teguise, a number of interesting rural museums, the wine-producing zone and the stunning Fundación César Manrique.

Costa Teguise

Costa Teguise ❾ is the only resort north of Arrecife. You enter on the Avenida del Mar (about 14km/8 miles from the airport,

6km/4 miles from the capital), a broad road lined with squat palm trees and flanked by hotels and apartment blocks. The main street, Avenida de las Islas Canarias, parallel to the coast, is lined with commercial centres, small supermarkets, several clinics and a plethora of car-hire outlets.

Manrique designed the **Pueblo Marinero** at the southern end of the resort, and this is the most appealing part of the development. Low, whitewashed houses with blue or green balconies are clustered in narrow streets around a small square, and it does genuinely resemble a fishing village – which is what Pueblo Marinero means. Later construction, running down to the beach, was taken over by other, less purist hands. A clutch of restaurants and bars here offer fish and chips, hamburgers and pizza, and many have English names. Round the rocky headland there are more buildings going up, and there's a small beach, **Playa del Jablillo**, with a rather unlovely view of the desalination plant just outside Arrecife.

Running northwards, the **Playa de las Cucharas** and **Playa de los Charcos** merge. The former has the better beach, a long stretch of golden imported sand superimposed on the natural volcanic black, and a stretch that is popular with windsurfers, as the winds on this coast are often strong. There is sand on Playa de los Charcos, too, but here there are black rocks to clamber over between sand and sea.

A landscaped promenade runs the length of the beaches, with a scattering of cafés and restaurants, and passes the smart Hotel Meliá Salinas, designed by Manrique, which in the 1970s became the first to be built here. The early ambitions for Costa Teguise have not been realised; it lacks a real heart and is more downmarket than the other two major resorts. As a base for exploring the island, however, it has its advantages, as it is very convenient for visiting the cultural sites and villages in the north and centre of Lanzarote.

Fundación César Manrique

From the *circunvalación* around Arrecife the LZ1 leads some 5km (3 miles) to **Tahiche**, where, on the outskirts, you will find the **Fundación César Manrique** ❿ (www.fcmanrique.org; daily 10am–6pm). This was the artist's home, which he remodelled as a museum and gallery when creating the foundation in 1982. All is white: outside, paths and walls gleam like icing sugar on a cake; inside, the marble floors blend with the white walls. Huge windows give views over the surrounding landscape, where the coils of molten lava look as if they might still be liquid. The

Colour-coded

Building materials and paint for external surfaces in Lanzarote are only available in brown, green and blue, the designated colours for woodwork on the white buildings.

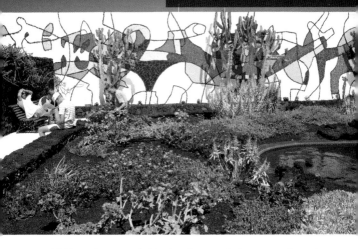

exhibition salons contain Manrique's own paintings, ceramics and sketches, as well as works by Picasso, Tàpies and Miró. Steps lead down to a series of volcanic bubbles, where trees reach up for the light. A subterranean garden has a pool and retains the atmosphere of a private home, with a huge barbecue and benches built into the walls. As you leave the building you pass through a small garden with a central pond and fountain, and a huge abstract mural that is one of Lanzarote's iconic sights.

Rural Heartland

About 8km (5 miles) west of the foundation you come to the sleepy little town of **San Bartolomé**. The parish church (often closed), the Teatro Municipal and the Ayuntamiento (Town Hall) form two sides of an attractive square with a colonnade, palm trees and a central fountain. Opposite, an open-ended plaza, planted with palms, cacti and oleanders, leads, via broad steps, down to the

Remnants of a bygone age in El Patio Museum

Museo Tanit (www.museotanit.com; Mon–Sat 10am–2pm), an ethnographic museum that outlines the history of the island's earliest inhabitants and has displays on two centuries of island life. The sculpture of two local dancers at the plaza commemorates their achievements in international competitions.

A right turn from the outskirts of San Bartolomé takes you the short distance to **Mozaga** ⑪ and the **Monumento del Campesino** (Monument to the Countryman; www.cactlanzarote.com), which is set in the exact centre of the island. Manrique's huge white sculpture depicts the *campesino*, surrounded, on the four compass points, by a camel, a donkey, a dog and a goat – although the abstract nature of the construction means that you need a bit of imagination to discern their figures.

Beside the monument a collection of attractive white buildings with green shutters comprise a café (daily 10am–5.45pm) and restaurant (daily noon–4pm) and the **Centro de Artesanía** (daily

10am–5.45pm; free). You can skirt around the restaurant to reach the artisans' centre, but don't – if you enter via the huge, domed structure you go through a rocky tunnel and a cool grotto to reach your destination. On the ground floor around a square are workshops where demonstrations of weaving, leather-working and pottery take place. Upstairs a small museum displays models of Lanzarote's early *ermitas* (chapels) and some excellent Naïve ceramic works.

The road leads north from the monument towards **Tiagua** ⓬. On the far side of the village you reach a tiny white *ermita*, and a right turn leads to the **Museo Agrícola El Patio** (www.museoelpatio. com; Mon–Fri 10am–5pm, Sat 10am–2.30pm). A museum of agriculture might not be your first idea of fun, but this one is a delight. On a small estate, once a rural centre where corn was brought to be milled, a fascinating collection of agricultural and domestic objects (complete with some spooky figures, their faces made from gourds) has been gathered. Set in grounds where chicken scratch in the dust and a donkey, goat and camel keep the farmyard theme alive, the museum is housed in a farmhouse dating from 1840 and a large converted barn. Perhaps the most interesting of the displays are numerous old photos, dating from the early 20th century to the 1960s, depicting the hardships and the community spirit of rural life. Leaving the museum, you pass through the old bodega, where you will be offered a glass of local wine. A quotation on the museum wall by Tenerife-born writer Agustín Espinosa (1897–1939) reads: 'A land without traditions, without a poetic atmosphere, faces the threat of extinction.' This place is doing all it can to keep those traditions and atmosphere alive.

Teguise

Villa de Teguise ⓭ was the first colonial capital of the island, built in the centre in the hope that it would be safe from pirate attacks. As you will learn if you visit the Castillo de Santa Bárbara (see page 48), this was not the case, but 'the royal town', as it was known, remained the capital until 1852. It is an attractive place, a village more than a town, with cobbled streets and a number of well-restored colonial buildings with typical Canarian wooden balconies and pretty courtyards.

Sunday is **market day** (9am–2pm) in Teguise, and tourists from all over the island descend on the little town – coach tours run from all the resorts. If you come by car, a series of car parks on the approach to town make life easy; attendants collect a small fee. The market sprawls all over Teguise, and there's a lively atmosphere, although you won't find much that you couldn't get in tourist shops and markets in any resort in Europe. Even the food on sale in the stalls and kiosks tends towards hamburgers, doughnuts and pizza rather than anything local. There are several good restaurants, though, where you can find Canarian food (see page 118), and a number of shops with more interesting goods: aloe vera products of all kinds are sold in several places, as are local cheeses, wine and jars of *mojo* sauce, a few ceramics and woven goods. Around midday there is a 30-minute exhibition of *lucha canaria* (see page 82) in the village centre, and performances of Canarian music by traditionally dressed local folkloric groups.

Teguise carnival

Teguise has a very lively carnival in February or early March, in which characters dressed as devils and brandishing goatskin truncheons attempt to terrorise carnival revellers.

There are three impressive churches in Teguise, two of them monastic, but despite advertised opening hours, you may not find them open. The **Convento de Santo Domingo** (Sun–Fri 10am–3pm, when there is an exhibition), founded by the

The popular market at Teguise

Dominican Order in 1698, has now become an art centre, which holds regular exhibitions of contemporary work. The church itself is worth a look: it has two naves, and the chapel dedicated to the Virgen del Rosario is the only one in Lanzarote where the retrochoir (the area directly behind the altar) features painted murals.

The **Convento de San Francisco** (Tue–Sat 9.30am–4.30pm, Sun 9am–2pm) founded by Franciscans in the late 16th century, houses a museum of sacred art with an interesting collection of religious paintings from 13th and 18th century. If it is closed you will have to be content with admiring the splendid main doorway. The **Iglesia de Nuestra Señora de Guadalupe** is an eclectic mixture of styles, having been remodelled many times during its long history, following pirate attacks and fires. Again, you may not find it open, but do not despair – Teguise has some great domestic architecture, especially the **Casa-Museo del Timple** in the **Palacio Spínola** (http://casadeltimple.org; Mon–Sat 9am–4pm, Sun 9am–3pm), which is a delight. Built for an aristocratic family in the mid-18th century, it was purchased by the local authorities and restored in the 1970s to become the official residence of the Canary Islands Autonomous Government. In 2011, it became a museum dedicated to the local history and to the *timple*, a traditional five-string instrument typical of the island. A series of beautifully furnished rooms, with wide, polished floorboards, beamed ceilings and lattice-work balconies and cupboards, is arranged around an internal patio, bright with bougainvillea, and an external one shaded by a huge fig tree.

The second of Teguise's palaces, now a small gallery for the works of local artists, is the **Palacio de Herrera y Rojas** (Mon–Sat 10am–1.30pm when there is an exhibition). The **Palacio del Marqués** with its elegant dining room and shady patio is another.

A final place to visit lies just outside Teguise (take a right turn from the main road and drive up a steep but well-surfaced road). This is the **Castillo de Santa Bárbara** ⑭, set on the top of the long-extinct Volcán de Guanapay. Built in the mid-16th century, this imposing building gave refuge to the people of Teguise and the surrounding countryside during repeated attacks by Turkish, French and English pirates. One particularly ferocious attack left the streets of Teguise running with blood – there is a street called the Callejón de la Sangre (Alley of Blood) – the island ransacked and the people starving. The castle is now home to the **Museo de la Piratería** (www.museodela pirateria.com; daily 10am–4pm) telling the stories of the biggest raids experienced by the island and of famous pirates such as John Hawkins, Francis Drake and Robert Blake.

The Casa-Museo Palacio Spínola in Teguise

Convento de San Francisco

Tinajo

From Teguise a road leads 5km (3 miles) northwest to **Tinajo**. The **Iglesia de San Roque** has statues by José Luján Pérez (1756–1815), the renowned Canarian sculptor. However, you must take your chances on finding it open. Nearby, the village of **Mancha Blanca** is best known for the **Ermita de los Dolores**. Inside is a statue of Nuestra Señora de los Volcanes, who is credited with saving the village by halting the lava flow from a volcanic eruption in 1824. Even if the church is closed, the snowy-white exterior is very pretty. The peace of the village is only disturbed on 15 September when a pilgrimage (*romería*) brings people from all over the island, and a craft fair, the Feria Insular de Artesanía Tradicional, is held. From here it's a very short distance to the Timanfaya National Park Visitors' Centre, but this is best saved for a separate visit to the park (see page 54).

The Rocky Coast

Instead, go north to La Santa, a village on the rocky coast that has prospered because of the proximity of the **Club La Santa** (www.clublasanta.co.uk). With facilities for 64 Olympic sports, the club has a vast stadium, an Olympic-sized pool, an artificial lake for windsurfing, and plenty of facilities for people of all abilities (or none), as well as those designed for training serious international sportspeople. If you want to visit the fishing village of **La Caleta de Famara**, the only other settlement on this coast, you must go back to Tiagua (about 12km/8 miles) and take another road north. There are a few good fish restaurants here and an excellent sandy beach, but strong winds make it unsafe for swimming.

Back at the centre of the island (the Monumento del Campesino is an excellent marker), a road runs southwest through **La Geria** wine country. You could stop at the **Bodega El Grifo Museo del Vino** (www.elgrifo.com; daily 10.30am–6pm, mid-July–mid-Sept until 7pm; guided tours daily 1pm and 4.30pm, booking required). Set in an old bodega, the museum exhibits wine-making equipment and has a good display on barrel-making; and, of course, there's wine for sale. Next door to El Grifo is the **Bodega Barreto**, owned by the oldest wine-producing family on the island. There

Club La Santa

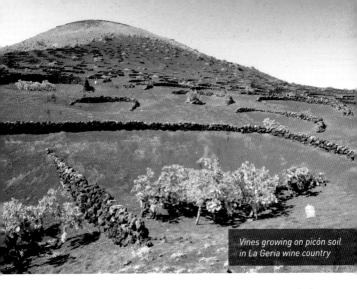

Vines growing on picón soil in La Geria wine country

is no museum here, but you can sample and purchase their wine. Drive on through the landscape of coiled lava and vineyards, where the vines growing in the *picón* (cinders) are planted within semicircles of volcanic rocks to stop the soil blowing away in Lanzarote's strong winds. This road will take you to Uga and the Parque Nacional de Timanfaya (see page 54).

Puerto del Carmen

Lying just 5km (3 miles) west of the airport, **Puerto del Carmen** ⓰ is Lanzarote's biggest resort. Its splendid beaches, Playa Grande and Playa de los Pocillos, and the less popular Playa Matagorda (closest to the airport), extend eastwards for 6km (4 miles) from the little fishing harbour that was the heart of the original village.

Until the 1970s this was just a quiet fishing community, and the area around the pretty harbour retains its village atmosphere. There is a little church here, **Nuestra Señora del Carmen**, but you will only find the doors open for Mass (Sat 8pm, Sun 11am and 7pm). There are numerous fish restaurants, too, mostly with excellent views. You can still see fish being unloaded from small fishing smacks by the jetty, but these vessels have been joined by leisure craft and excursion boats offering trips around the coast and across to Fuerteventura. The little rocky coves just east of the harbour, before the beaches begin, are popular with divers.

The golden sands of **Playa Grande**, lined with sunbeds (hamacas) and bright umbrellas for rent, offer all kinds of diversions – banana boats, pedalos in the shape of giant swans, beach cafés and, of couse, glorious waters. Parallel to the beach is the **Avenida de las Playas**. Along the sea-side runs an attractive promenade, planted with palms and flowering shrubs. Here you'll find a helpful little **tourist office** (daily 10am–6pm), next door to a small gift shop belonging to the Fundación Manrique, as well as Lanzarote's only **casino**, a couple of nice restaurants, and a few little villa complexes. On the other side, the avenue resembles a vast amusement arcade, lined with cafés, bars and restaurants – mostly with Irish or English names, advertising Guinness, fish and chips and all-day English breakfasts – along with tourist-oriented shops and kiosks offering tattos and hair-braiding. At intervals there are centros comerciales, with more shops and restaurants, and it is here that most of the late-night bars and clubs are found. Just past a rocky headland, the Punta de Barranquillo, these commercial outlets peter out, to be replaced with smart little residential complexes. Then, where the **Playa de los Pocillos** commences, so do more shops and bars, but these are far more low-key than the earlier ones.

Puerto Calero is named after the developer José Calero, who initiated the construction of the marina in 1986. It lies about 4km (2.5 miles) south of Puerto del Carmen and styles itself a puerto deportivo – a sports port. Its smart harbour is full of sleek yachts, its restaurants full of sleek people. You can charter a boat if you fancy a day's deep-sea fishing (see page 84). If you're just dropping in for a look around, it's easiest to take a boat trip from Puerto del Carmen, so you don't have to worry about parking, which can be a problem.

A short drive on LZ505 north of Puerto Carmen lies a small town of Tías which has a small but interesting museum, **A Casa José Saramago** ⑯ (Calle Los Topes 2; http://acasajosesaramago. com; Mon–Sat 10am–2.30pm, last entry at 1.30pm), located in the house where the late Nobel-winning Portuguese writer spent much of the last 18 years of his life. Visitors can walk around this simple but finely furnished house preserved just as the author of *Blindness* left it and enjoy fabulous views over a cup of excellent Portuguese coffee (included in the ticket price) served on the garden terrace. There is also a wonderful library and museum shop with Saramago books in many languages and other souvenirs.

THE SOUTH

The south of Lanzarote encompasses the extraordinary volcanic wilderness of the Parque Nacional de Timanfaya, the pretty, arty village of Yaiza, Playa Blanca with its splendid beaches, and the wild jagged coast to the west.

Parque Nacional de Timanfaya

Going south from the airport, take the LZ2 motorway towards Tías, from where a straight stretch continues to Yaiza (about 18km/11 miles). Just before Yaiza lies the little village of **Uga**, looking like a Moorish settlement, with flat-roofed white houses surrounded by palms. About 3km (2 miles) further on a bypass encircles Yaiza. From a roundabout as you approach is a narrow road leading to the **Parque Nacional de Timanfaya** ❶ and Centro de Interpretación de Mancha Blanca (daily 9am–4.30pm). On the way up you pass the **Echadero de Camellos**

⊙ VISITING TIMANFAYA NATIONAL PARK

At the entrance to the park, where Manrique's famous 'fire devil' sign stands, is a barrier, where you pay an entrance fee. You will probably have to join a queue while you wait for a space to become available in the car park, from where buses take visitors on a 40-minute tour of the Ruta de los Volcanes. At busy times – late morning seems to be prime time – the wait may be as long as an hour. Take drinking water and something to amuse the children when they get bored. You are not allowed to walk, or drive, through the centre of the park, but you can drive around the periphery, and drop in to the Visitors' Centre at the Tinajo end. Any cars you see going straight ahead instead of waiting at the barrier are doing just that.

(Camel Station; daily 9am–5pm) where visitors are taken for rides around the outer volcanic slopes on dromedaries. There is also a small museum of volcanic rocks here. The national park is one place that all visitors to Lanzarote should include on their itineraries.

Bus tours around the **Montañas del Fuego** (Mountains of Fire; www.cactlanzarote.com; daily 9am–5.45pm, July–Sept until 6.45pm) start from outside El Diablo restaurant and run throughout the day. There is a good recorded commentary in Spanish, English and German, giving background information about the park and about the volcanic eruptions that caused this once fertile area to be turned into a sea of lava. There are frequent photo stops at particularly dramatic points, but you are not allowed to get off the bus. Once the tour is over, most visitors stop for a while to watch park attendants throwing dried brush into a hole in the ground, whereupon flames roar upwards; or pouring buckets of water into a small crater, causing a cascade of boiling water to shoot into the air.

In the glass-sided restaurant (daily noon–3.45pm), designed, of course, by César Manrique, you can have a drink or snack, or eat meat that has been grilled over the natural heat emanating from just below the surface (you can watch chefs officiating over the barbecue at the back of the restaurant, so you know that they are not cheating). There is also a café (9am–4.50pm) and a small artisan shop.

Yaiza

The visit over, return to the roundabout and take the road straight into **Yaiza** ⓲. This village relishes its reputation as the prettiest on Lanzarote – and it certainly is extremely picturesque. Some typically Canarian-style buildings survived the eruption that wiped out most of the village in the 1730s, and these have been complemented by later ones in the same style. Palms line the road as you approach, scarlet geraniums decorate green balconies and bougainvillea drips over snowy-white garden walls.

In the central square is the church of **Nuestra Señora de los Remedios**, which has columns of volcanic rock and a beautiful painted wooden ceiling; unlike many of the island churches, it is usually open. By contrast the **Galería Yaiza** (Mon-Sat 5–7pm; free), at the west end of the village, has good exhibitions of contemporary art, but the limited opening hours mean you have to make a special effort to see them.

Yaiza has several nice places to stay and a couple of good restaurants (see pages 120 and 140), including the renowned **La Era** (www.laera.com), set in an 18th-century farmhouse converted by Manrique.

One of Playa Blanca's golden beaches

Playa Blanca

The road from Yaiza leads south, through the bare, flat lands called El Rubicón, to **Playa Blanca** ⑲. This is Lanzarote's third resort, smaller, quieter and more upmarket than the other two. It used to be a flourishing fishing village, and retains something of that atmosphere, even as it has expanded.

The heart of the resort centres on the main street, Avenida de Papagayo, its pedestrianised extension, Calle Limones, and the Paseo Marítimo, a promenade lined with restaurants that runs parallel to the soft sands of **Playa Dorada** (Golden Beach) and **Playa Blanca** (White Beach) and leads to the port. West of the port, another tree-lined promenade runs round the Punta Limones headland to pretty little Playa Flamingo, backed by landscaped gardens, and with calm, safe waters. Across a narrow stretch of the Atlantic, the sands of Corralejo, on Fuerteventura, gleam in the sunlight.

Playa Blanca is big on water sports and all kinds of maritime excursions, whether you want to scuba dive, windsurf or simply take a trip in a glass-bottomed submarine (see pages 83 and 85). The extraordinary **Museo Atlántico** (www.cactlanzarote.com), an underwater museum conceived by British-born sculptor Jason deCaires Taylor, is located at a depth of 12m (39ft) in the Bahía de las Coloradas. Made of pH-neutral cement, the sculptures form an artificial reef and a surreal underwater world waiting to be explored by divers. Visits must be organised with a certified diving company, such as Calipso Diving or Manta Diving (see page 83).

How long Playa Blanca will retain its fishing-village atmosphere is hard to say. Already, *urbanizaciones* stretch to the left and right (where most of the big hotels and villa complexes are situated), and on the approach to the village new buildings are going up fast, although there has been a great deal of controversy about the speed and extent of the developments. To the east of town, new roads lead to the **Marina Rubicón**, a swish sports complex, with a 400-berth marina surrounded by

⊘ PARTICLES OF PERIDOT

The glimmers and glitters you will notice in the black-sand beach at El Golfo come from tiny particles of peridot, a semi-precious stone that is also called olivine, and ranges in colour from olive to lime-green. You will see peridot necklaces and bracelets for sale all over the island. It is the August birth-stone and is believed to bring good luck. The stones used to be called evening emeralds, and it is said that the crusaders, who found them around the Red Sea, believed they were emeralds and brought them back home to adorn churches.

Part of the crater shell, El Golfo

apartments, a huge shopping and leisure centre with tennis courts and a pool, plentiful bars and restaurants, and the five-star Hotel Volcán Lanzarote (see page 139).

Further east, in a protected area known as **Los Ajaches**, lie Lanzarote's best beaches – **Playa de las Mujeres** and **Playa del Papagayo** ⑳. Be cautious about driving along the dirt road that gives access to them: insurance on hired cars does not cover you for 'off-road' driving, and the emergency services will not come and get you if you run into trouble. If you do drive, note that there is a small toll (currently €3). It's easier, and more pleasant, to take the *Princess Yaiza* Taxi Boat (tel: 928 514 322/629 731 293), which leaves four times a day from the harbour and the Marina Rubicón.

Salinas de Janubio and El Golfo

Parallel to the main road from Yaiza is another, the 701, which branches off westwards to the **Salinas de Janubio** ㉑.

Salt production was one of the most important industries in Lanzarote, its main purpose being to preserve fish rather than for domestic use. These salt pans are the only ones still in use and they are an impressive sight, laid out like a patchwork quilt, the colour of each pan depending on the relative amount of water and salt it contains. They are also an excellent spot for birdwatching, especially during the spring and autumn migratory periods.

A short way further up this rocky, deeply eroded coast is a spot known as **Los Hervideros** (The Boiling Pans). You will see coaches in the large car park, for this is a stopping point for tours coming from Timanfaya. It gained its name because the seething sea appears to boil in blowholes and underwater lava caves created by a volcanic tube emerging into the sea. Continue up the coast (where there are plenty of lay-bys to allow drivers to stop and admire the craggy coastline) and you soon arrive at **El Golfo**, a fishing village set between volcanic hills and pounding sea. It's just a collection of pretty cottages and fish restaurants, with outside tables by the sea. To the southern side of the village, the shell of a volcanic crater has been eroded into a jagged, richly coloured cliff. At its foot lie a small black beach and a vivid green **lagoon**, also called El Golfo. Park at the entrance to the village and follow a footpath in order to find it.

From El Golfo the 702 leads back to Yaiza, from where you pick up the main road back towards Arrecife and the airport.

FUERTEVENTURA

On arriving at the coast of Fuerteventura in 1402, Jean de Béthencourt reputedly exclaimed '¡Que aventura más fuerte!' (What a great adventure!). That's one theory about the origin of the island's name. Others, more prosaically, believe it derives from *viento fuerte* – strong wind. Winds are certainly a feature of the island, and one that draws surfers, windsurfers, kitesurfers and parasailors to its gorgeous sandy beaches: the long stretches in the north, around El Cotillo and at Corralejo, now protected in a Parque Natural; and in the south, the sands stretch from Tarajalejo to Morro Jable and beyond. But there is more to Fuerteventura than beaches: the sleepy little towns in the interior are

Fuerteventura's desert landscape

keepers of the island's history, places where life goes on pretty much as it has for centuries. We begin with the capital, then travel north before visiting the centre and south of the island.

THE NORTH

The north of the island is a diverse area that encompasses the capital, Puerto del Rosario; a number of inland towns and villages, set amid bare conical hills, where you can learn about the agricultural past; and the harbours, dunes and beaches of Corralejo to the east and El Cotillo in the west.

Puerto del Rosario

Puerto del Rosario ❶ lies about 7km (4 miles) north of the airport. The town was founded in 1795, called Puerto de Cabras (Goat Port), and became the island capital in 1860 (taking over the role from La Oliva). The name was changed in 1956, but the goat motif is evident in statuary and in a pastoral metallic mural. A small, busy port is used by ferries from Arrecife, container ships and cruise liners. Puerto del Rosario is not a tourist-oriented town, but is worth a brief visit. The harbour front is a pleasant place to walk. Palms offer shade along the inland side, and the sea wall is lined with sinuous benches decorated with coloured tiles. An area designated the Parque de Mayores is a kind of outdoor gym for elderly people, with a variety of exercise machines and notices warning of the dangers of over-exertion.

The town is known for its **street sculpture**, which ranges from a huge fountain on a roundabout on the Avenida Marítima, to an abstract metallic clock in the centre of town, to two naked dancing women in a square, and simple statues dotted all over the place – a fisherman stands on the sea wall, while an elderly man sits outside the church.

It was the church, dedicated to the **Virgen del Rosario,** that gave the town its new name. It's a simple grey-and-white building, somewhat neglected, standing in a tree-shaded square opposite the island government offices. To the side of the square is the **Casa-Museo Unamuno** (Mon–Fri 9am–2pm; www.artesaniaymuseosdefuerteventura.org), the house (then the Hotel Fuerteventura) where the Basque writer and philosopher

Stone fisherman by the sea

Miguel de Unamuno (1864–1936) lived when he was exiled here in 1924, regarded as a thorn in the flesh of Miguel Primo de Rivera's dictatorship. Unamuno's time here was brief, but he quickly came to love the island and to appreciate the kindness shown to him by local people. They later reciprocated by erecting a huge statue of him on the lower flanks of Montaña Quemada (Burnt Mountain), just outside Tindaya. The rooms are furnished as they were in Unamuno's time, with portraits and memorabilia, and quotations from his writing are displayed on the walls.

Weaving at La Alcogida

At the roundabout where roads into Puerto del Rosario meet, stands **Las Rotondas**, (http://lasrotondascentrocomercial.com/es) a huge commercial centre that adds greatly to the town's previously rather limited shopping opportunities with a range of internationally known stores.

Farms and Windmills

From Puerto del Rosario the FV10 runs northwest towards La Oliva. En route, a left turn is clearly signposted to **Tefia** ❷ and the **Ecomuseo La Alcogida** (Tue–Sat 10am–5.30pm; www.artesaniay museosdefuerteventura.org). This ingenious complex, which stretches out on either side of the road, is an abandoned farming settlement that has been restored as a museum, and allows visitors to see how rural life was lived, and what farming methods were used, during the last century. You can watch people demonstrating pulled-thread embroidery, basket-work, leather-work and weaving, and try their home-made aniseed bread.

Just past the museum a road leads off to **Los Molinos** – passing, after a few hundred metres, a beautifully restored windmill, which is visible from La Alcogida. Los Molinos is a pretty little seaside village, with a couple of nice restaurants, about 8km (5 miles) west. Returning to the main road and going north, you pass, on your left, **Montaña Quemada** ❸, where Unamuno's statue blends with its craggy background; a little further on is the cheese-producing town of Tindaya and **Montaña Tindaya** (397m/1,303ft), which the island's indigenous people considered a sacred mountain.

La Oliva

You soon come to **La Oliva** ❹. This sleepy little town was the seat of the Guanche king, Guixe, and briefly served as the colonial capital of the island in the early 18th century. Today, it's a workaday

⊙ CHILLIDA'S DREAM

In 1992 the Basque sculptor Eduardo Chillida put forward an ambitious proposal to create within Montaña Tindaya a vast open space. Nothing would be visible externally, but within the artist hoped to realise 'a utopia... where those who went inside would be able to see the light of the sun, the moon, to see the sea and the horizon...' The Cabildo Insular supported the plan, but there was a great deal of opposition from environmentalists. Whether or not the project would have gone ahead is unknown, as Chillida died in 2002.

Canarian Art Centre in La Oliva

town, centred on a large church, **Nuestra Señora de Candelaria**, with buttressed walls and a square bell tower of volcanic stone. The interior is quite plain, and the pulpit, decorated with pictures of the four Apostles, is supported on a slim, painted pedestal (1 in a slot by the door gives five minutes' worth of illumination).

From the side of the Ayuntamiento, opposite the church, a straight, broad road leads to the **Casa de los Coroneles** (House of the Colonels; www.lacasadeloscoroneles.org; Tue–Sat 10am–6pm). This grandiose and much-photographed building, with its many balconied windows, was the seat of the military rulers of the island in the early 18th century. After undergoing extensive restoration is now a cultural centre where exhibitions and concerts are held.

En route to the colonels' headquarters you pass the **Centro de Arte Canario** (http://centrodeartecanario.com; Mon–Fri 10am–5pm, Sat 10am–2pm) in the Casa Mané, a converted colonial

La Rosita provides a glimpse of traditional rural life

house. The collection of works by contemporary Canarian, or Canary Island-based, artists is somewhat eclectic, and the sculpture in the extensive cactus garden even more so, ranging from innovative abstract pieces to leaping dolphins and even some (possibly ironic) gnomes. Don't miss the galleries situated down a flight of steps and through the shop, as this is where some of the best work is shown, in large, light rooms.

Villaverde and Lajares

From the centre of La Oliva the FV10 leads towards the northwest coast, but it may be worth taking the slightly longer way round (up the FV101 then turning onto the FV109), because you could then stop at **Villaverde** to see the **Cueva del Llano** ❺ (tel: 928 175 928; Wed–Thu 10am–5pm and Sat 3–5.30pm, summer Tue–Sat 10am–6pm; currently closed due for safety reasons). This *jameo*, or lava tube, was discovered in 1979, and a new species of spider,

Arácnido triglobio, was found to be living here. A visitors' centre offers information about the *jameo,* which was formed by a lava stream from nearby Montaña Escanfraga. A few kilometres north is **La Rosita** (Mon–Sat 10am–6pm), a farm that demonstrates traditional agricultural methods, including the use of camels on the land. Children especially enjoy contact with the farm animals.

Just before the FV109 joins the FV10 to El Cotillo, you reach **Lajares**, a village with a pair of well-restored windmills on the southern outskirts, and a stadium where *lucha canaria* (see page 82) is performed. In the main street is the **Escuela de Artesanía** (Mon–Fri 9am–7pm, Sat 9am–3pm). Although called a school, it is really more of a shop, where you can buy handmade products (not cheap) and watch local women embroidering table linen.

El Cotillo

The road continues about 8km (5 miles) to **El Cotillo** ❻. This village has a gloriously pretty little fishing harbour and a selection of good fish restaurants to go with it, plus beautiful, wind-swept dunes and beaches.

Beside the harbour is the **Castillo de Tostón** (Mon–Fri 9am–3pm, Sat–Sun 9am–2pm), a sturdy fortress that houses a small gallery (same hours) with changing exhibitions of work by local artists. El Cotillo has a small but vibrant artistic community, with some French connections. From the fort's roof you get wonderful views down the coast. To the north, a narrow road runs through the dunes to the Punta de Tostón, where a lighthouse stands on a headland. A lot of construction work is going on in El Cotillo, and it is to be hoped that the character of the village won't be spoiled.

Corralejo

Return to the main FV101 and after about 6km (4 miles) you reach **Corralejo** ❼. (You may have started here, having come, as many do, by boat from Playa Blanca in Lanzarote; (see page 135). Corralejo is another tiny fishing village that has expanded to cope with the demand for tourist accommodation. The heart of the town, the area around the harbour, still has a character of its own. On **Muelle Chico** (Small Jetty) there's a **tourist information kiosk** (Mon–Fri 7.45am–3pm, Sat–Sun 9am–3pm) close to a bronze statue called the **Monumento Marinero**, showing a returned sea-man embracing his wife and child; nearby, another woman looks out to sea, waiting for her husband's return. The narrow lanes that radiate from the harbour and the broad main street, Nuestra Señora del Carmen, filled with cafés, bars and shops, are remi-niscent of an English seaside resort, and not just because most of the voices you hear are English. There is also something of a hippy-ish, beachcomber feel here, generated by the people who come in search of good waves and a laid-back lifestyle.

In Corralejo you can go diving and scuba diving, take a beach-buggy trip through the dunes to El Cotillo, hire a mountain bike, go on a dolphin-watching boat ride or, most popular of all, take a trip to **Isla de Lobos ❽** (Island of Wolves). The wolves in question were the sea lions that flourished here before they were devoured by Norman sailors who came to the island with Gadifer de la Salle's invasion force (see page 16). It's a peaceful, pretty place, unin-habited, although you'll have to share it with lots of other visitors, and it's small enough to walk around in about three hours. You can see sea birds – Cory's sheerwaters nest here – and a variety of vegetation in spring and early summer. The waters are sheltered and safe even for children to swim, so it is well worth bringing a picnic and spending a day here.

The Dunes

Drive out of town on the FV1, which runs parallel to the coast through great swathes of **El Jable dunes** that are now protected

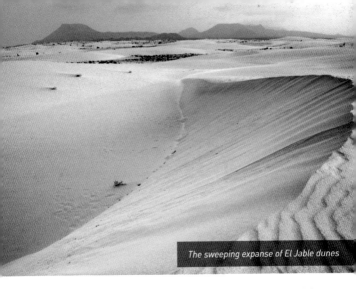

The sweeping expanse of El Jable dunes

as the **Parque Natural de Corralejo** ❾. Look out for goats, which sometimes wander onto the road. On the edge of, but just inside, the park looms the huge Riu Palace Tres Islas Hotel (www.riu. com), built before strict planning controls made such construction illegal. Thereafter, there's little more to it than sand and more sand, low brown hills to the right, and a gorgeous sweep of turquoise waters to your left, crashing against the 10km (6 miles) of beach that draw water sports enthusiasts in droves.

The road runs some 35km (22 miles) back to Puerto del Rosario, from where you can begin a tour of the centre and south of the island.

THE CENTRE
Visiting the central part of the island offers the contrast of starting out on the coast at Caleta de Fuste, a smart, purpose-built holiday resort, then heading inland to Fuerteventura's

first capital, Betancuria, and a number of other pretty towns and villages, set amid stunning mountain scenery and the occasional fertile valley.

Caleta de Fuste

Some 7km (4 miles) south of Puerto del Rosario and 9km (6 miles) south of the airport, on the FV2, lies **Caleta de Fuste** ⑩. This is a completely made-to-measure resort, clustered around a marina and the Castillo de Fuste, the 18th-century fortress from which it takes its name, and spreading inland and along the coast. Opinions are divided on Caleta de Fuste: on the one hand, it has the artificial feel of a resort created from scratch; on the other, it has been well-designed, and there's a range of accommodation, good restaurants, and water sports and activities of all kinds, as well as a pleasant sandy beach. The Barceló Club El Castillo (www.barcelo.com), in a prime site right by the beach, is a nicely landscaped complex of attractive bungalows that resembles an entire village. To the north, a broad promenade leads along the rocky shore to Costa de Antigua; to the south, construction is going on apace up to and around the garish Centro Atlántico shopping centre (www.ccatlanticofuerteventura.com).

Follow the road a short way south to **Las Salinas** to visit the **Museo de la Sal** (Salt Museum; Tue–Sat 10am–6pm; www.artesaniaymuseosdefuerteventura.org) and the surrounding salt pans, the **Salinas del**

Stop for a view

Just past Antigua the FV416 goes off to the left towards Betancuria. En route, if you want a stunning view over the khaki-coloured landscape and undulating hills, stop at the Mirador Morro Velosa, where there is a small coffee and craft shop and viewing area, designed by César Manrique.

Carmen, and learn about the extraction of salt.

Antigua

The road turns inland from here, and after about 10km (6 miles) the FV50 leads off to **Antigua** ⓫, set in the very middle of the island. Antigua used to be an important commercial centre and was briefly the capital of Fuerteventura (1834–5). Today it's a quiet town, centred on its sturdy church, **Nuestra Señora**

Antigua's windmill

de Antigua, one of the oldest on the island. It stands in a huge paved square, to one side of which a smaller grassy area, the **Plaza de los Caídos**, features a large cross, commemorating those who died in the Civil War. The church has a wooden ceiling and a wide nave, and is largely unadorned apart from a brightly painted main altar.

On the town's northern outskirts is the **Molino de Antigua Centro de Artesanía**, which houses the **Museo del Queso Majorero** (Majorero Cheese Museum; Tue–Sat 10am–6pm). This is a fascinating complex of buildings, set in pleasant gardens, with a collection of cacti. There is a windmill, where you can see the machinery used to grind *gofio* and an exhibition on the art of cheese making and cattle breeding, both typical of the island. There is craftwork on sale, too, comprising textiles, woven baskets and hats, and reproductions of Majorero ceramics.

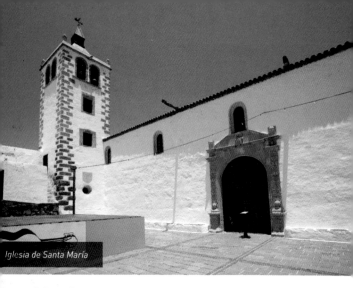

Iglesia de Santa María

Betancuria

Betancuria ⑫ is a little jewel of a town, with scarcely a corner that is not picturesque, and it is well aware both of its prettiness and its historical importance. 'Six hundred years of history' announces a sign on the wall of the **Ayuntamiento** (Town Hall) – itself a delightful building with a courtyard you can pop into. This was Fuerteventura's first capital, founded in the early 15th century by Jean de Béthencourt when his original stronghold on the coast proved not strong enough to deter pirate attacks. You can still see the remains of the Franciscan Convento de San Buenaventura, which was established here so that the brothers who followed in the conqueror's wake could bring Christianity to the native people.

There are car parks at either end of the town, which you should use – you cannot drive into the village itself, although there is some roadside parking in the main street. Here you will find the **Museo Arqueológico y Etnográfico** (temporarily closed), with displays ranging from bones, fossils and some prized fertility idols to Majorero ceramics and information on the first colonisers.

Walk through the cobbled streets to the lovely **Iglesia de Santa María** (Mon–Sat 10am–5pm), which was consecrated in 1426, destroyed by pirates in 1593 and rebuilt a century later. Entrance to the church and the adjoining **Museo de Arte Sacra** usually alternates every half-hour, a rather odd arrangement but one that seems to work.

The church has an intricately carved door, a splendid wooden ceiling and a most unusual floor – large square stones outlined with wooden boards. The ceiling in the sacristy is of Mudéjar design, but decorated with a renaissance painting. There are some real treasures in both the church and the museum, including a lovely retable of La Inmaculada to the left of the high altar and numerous polychromatic wooden figures of saints, some of them salvaged from the convent. The oldest part of the church, the baptistery, has a Gothic ribbed vault.

Across the square from the church, attached to the Casa Santa María restaurant (see page 122), is the **Museo de Artesanía** (www.casasantamaria.

Museo de Artesanía

La Vega del Río de las Palmas

net; Mon–Sat 10am–3.30pm, restaurant open until 5.30pm),
arranged around a series of flower-filled courtyards. There
are lots of domestic and agricultural implements, women in
traditional costume demonstrating weaving, and lots of local
produce for sale at very reasonable prices. Sometimes there
are wine- and cheese-tastings included. Upstairs, you can
watch a short film about the island.

La Vega del Río de las Palmas and Pájara

You drop down now to the 'Valley of Palms', a surprisingly green
and fertile region of this dry island, where in mid-September
the village of **La Vega del Río de las Palmas** hosts a festival to
the Virgen de la Peña (Virgin of Sorrows), patron saint of the
island. The rest of the year it's a very sleepy place, but in its
main square stands an attractive sandstone **church**, built in
1666 and dedicated to the Virgin.

The road twists and turns on its way south, but it is well surfaced, and there's a protective barrier, and lots of lay-bys where you can stop to drink in the splendid views, take photographs, or just let an impatient driver pass you by.

When the road straightens out, you come to the pretty village of **Pájara** ⑬. Palms and oleanders line the main street leading to the church of **Nuestra Señora de la Regla** (daily 11am–1pm, 5–7pm), famous for its red sandstone doorway, carved with symbols that apear to be Aztec-influenced, including a figure with a plumed feather headdress. The church has two naves, each with a Baroque high altar – put 1 euro in the box by the door to illuminate them.

Outside the church is a water pump with a long wooden 'arm' to which a camel used to be attached to do the heavy work of pulling up the water. To the side of the church, an attractive park, bright with bougainvillea in summer, lines a dry riverbed. Leaving the village to the southeast, you pass a roundabout with a large sandstone statue depicting a farmer milking a goat.

Heading south now, the road rejoins the FV20 which will take you back to the capital or south to the beaches. Even if going south, you could, if you are interested in the island's famous windmills, make a slight detour to **Tiscamanita**

A detail from the doorway of Nuestra Señora de la Regla

where the **Centro de Interpretación Los Molinos** (Tue–Sat 10am–6pm) demonstrates the history of milling.

THE SOUTH

It is the beauty of the southern beaches, and the activities they offer, that bring most visitors to Fuerteventura. The combination of barren, elephant-coloured hills, jagged cliffs and great sweeps of white sand is irresistible, and the reliably strong winds promise windsurf enthusiasts the time of their lives. There are also some sheltered coves, though, ideal for those who simply want to enjoy the almost perpetual sunshine. The Sotavento (Leeward) beaches on the east side of the Jandía Peninsula are the most popular; the Barlovento (Windward) beaches on the other side are only for the most hardy and experienced windsurfers. These, and the far tip of the peninsula, Punta de Jandía, are accessible only on tracks that most car-hire companies' insurance will not cover.

Gran Tarajal and Tarajalejo

Gran Tarajal ⑭, reached by a straight stretch of road off the FV2, is the island's second-largest port, and therefore has a character of its own that has not been subsumed by the tourist resort that has grown up around it. Narrow streets lead away from a black-sand beach and a broad promenade, planted with palms and lined with restaurants.

From **Tarajalejo**, a little further down the coast, the main road parallels the shore. Tarajalejo is a fishing village that has developed into a resort but, although it is expanding rapidly, is still low-key and pleasant. It has a 1km (0.6-mile) pebbly beach and a large main square. The village is popular with sailing enthusiasts and caters well for beginners.

About 5km (3 miles) down the coast, just before the Barranco de Tarajal, lies **La Lajita**, a nice little village with a harbour. On

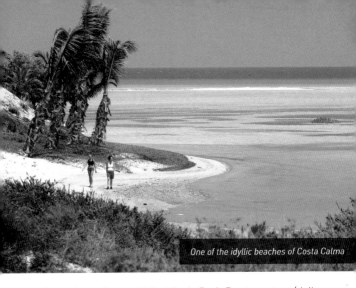
One of the idyllic beaches of Costa Calma

the main road you will find **Oasis Park** Fuerteventura (daily 9am–6pm; www.fuerteventuraoasispark.com) with camel rides, giraffes, reptiles, sea lions, parrots and birds of prey, as well as an impressive botanical garden. It's quite expensive, but it makes an enjoyable family day out.

Playas de Sotavento

A little further down the coast a secondary road leads 5km (3 miles) across the narrow neck of the peninsula to the village and beach of **La Pared** (don't ever windsurf here alone – the currents are very dangerous). A wall *(pared)*, built by the Majoreros, stretched across here when the conquerors arrived, and now it roughly forms the boundary of the **Parque Natural de Jandía**, some 14,320 hectares (35,385 acres) in extent, which reaches down to the tip of the peninsula.

Next, you come to **Costa Calma** ⑮ and the start of the long white beaches of Sotavento. Development at Costa Calma began in the 1970s and has expanded ever since, encompassing a variety of accommodation, most of it block-booked by German tour companies, with the hotels providing most of the restaurants and entertainment their guests need.

A little further south, on the beautiful **Playa Barca**, the huge Hotel Meliá Gorriones (see page 142) commands a prime position. It is here that the world's largest windsurfing centre, the Pro Center René Egli (www.rene-egli.com), is located, and where the PWA/ISA Windsurfing and the PKRA Kiteboarding World Championships are held in late July–early August. You don't have to be a champion to windsurf here, but you do have to be careful.

Continuing down this overdeveloped coast, you will come to **Playa de Matorral** (confusingly also known as Playa de Jandía), where the long white beach has been subject to a rash of huge hotels, apartment blocks, shops and restaurants. A section of the Matorral area has now been designated a Site of Special Scientific Interest, in an attempt to preserve the vegetation and varied bird life of its salt marshes, and an EU project has been launched to raise awareness of the damage that is being done by uncontrolled development. On the **Punta de Matorral** stands a lighthouse, with a beach bar at its feet.

Playa de Matorral merges with **Morro del Jable** ⑯, the southernmost resort on the peninsula – after this the concrete developments thin out. Morro del Jable is a town with a proper port, even though hotels and apartment blocks have stretched their

Ferry crossings

From Morro del Jable Naviera Armas (www.naviera armas.com) ferries run to Las Palmas de Gran Canaria seven times a week, taking about 2.5–3 hours.

tentacles up the hillsides behind it. There's an attractive seaside promenade, some good fish restaurants and opportunities for all kinds of watersports.

The North of the Peninsula

The roads beyond Morro del Jable down to Puerto de la Cruz and the Punta de Jandía, and round to Cofete on the northern side of the peninsula, are not to be recommended unless you have a four-

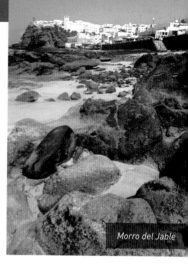

Morro del Jable

wheel-drive vehicle, and even then you should check the details of your insurance cover. There is no road going across the peninsula, just a ridge of mountains cut through with *barrancos* (gullies) and dominated by **Montaña de Jandía**, the highest peak on the island at 807m (2,648ft). The most common form of vegetation here is the *cardón de Jandía*, the symbol of Fuerteventura.

The beaches at the peninsula's tip and the **Playa de Cofete** and **Playa de Barlovento** (both favoured by nudists) on the other side are largely deserted, undeniably beautiful, and swept by high winds. Rocks are sculpted into jagged forms, sea spurge survives on the dunes, and a few goats are the only sign of wildlife. The tiny hamlet of Cofete is known only for the Villa Winter, an abandoned house built by a Nazi sympathiser on land allegedly given to him by General Franco. All kinds of rumours have surrounded this villa over the years, but this untamed region is just the sort of place in which rumours flourish and myths are created.

Windsurfing is popular on both islands

WHAT TO DO

Most of the things you can do on Lanzarote and Fuerteventura are done outdoors, many of them on or in the water. Ideal winds and waves make windsurfing the most popular activity, but there are many others – sailing, diving, fishing, swimming and lots of boat trips. On land, there are some good hiking trails, opportunities for horse riding and exploring the rougher terrain by jeep, buggy or quad bike safari, and plenty of activities for children.

SPORTS AND OUTDOOR ACTIVITIES

WINDSURFING

On **Lanzarote** the Windsurfing Club Las Cucharas (Centro Comercial las Maretas, Calle Marajo, Costa Teguise; tel: 928 590 731; www.lanzarotewindsurf.com) offers advanced, beginners' and children's courses, plus other activities (see page 88). Windsurf Paradise (Calle la Corvina 8, Playa de las Cucharas, Costa Teguis; tel: 657 641 107; www.windsurflanzarote.com), also offers lessons, from basic to advanced levels, and surfing trips to other beaches on the island.

On **Fuerteventura** a selection of operators includes Escuela de Windsurf El Castillo (Caleta de FusteFuste; tel: 928 163 100), Ventura Surf Center (Avenida Marítima 54, Correlejo; tel: 928 866 295; www.ventura-surf.com) and *the* name in windsurfing, Pro Center René Egli I (Hotel Meliá Gorriones, Playa Sotavento; tel: 928 547 483; www.rene-egli.com). There's a second centre, René Egli II, 3km (2 miles) further south, where winds are less strong and there is an area of shallow water more suitable for beginners.

KITESURFING

On **Fuerteventura** try the Fuerteventura Kiteboarding School (El Cotillo; tel: 928 538 504; www.ksfuerte.com) and Flag Beach Windsurf and Kitesurf Centre (tel: 928 866 389, mobile: 609 029 804; www.flagbeach.com) in Corralejo.

SURFING

Lanzarote surf schools include Calima Surf (Caleta de Famara; tel: 928 528 528; www.calimasurf.com), Surf School Lanzarote (Caleta de Famara; tel: 686 004 909, www.surfschoolanzarote. com), Famara Surf (Avenida El Marinero 39, Caleta de Famara; tel: 616 107 621; www.famarasurf.com) for classes at all levels plus equipment, and Windsurf Paradise (see page 81).

There is less surfing on **Fuerteventura**, but Ineika Funcenter (Corralejo; tel: 928 535 744; www.ineika.com) caters for beginners and advanced surfers, and arranges transfers to the best surf

⊙ LUCHA CANARIA

Lucha canaria is a popular sport that dates back to pre-Hispanic times. It is a form of wrestling in which members of two teams of 12 wrestlers take it in turns to throw an opponent to the ground. The bout *(brega)* is lost if any part of a wrestler's body (except his feet, of course) touches the ground. You are most likely to see the sport at village fiestas, and there is usually a demonstration in Teguise on Sunday market day, around noon. Another traditional local sport is *juego del palo*, or stick-fighting. The object is to keep the body as still as possible, while fending off the blows from an opponent's stave – a stick about 1.8m (6ft) long. Again, you are most likely to see one of these bouts at a village festival; ask at a local tourist office.

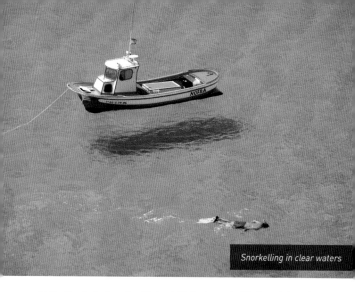

Snorkelling in clear waters

spots; the Quiksilver Surf School (Calle Anzuelo 23, Corralejo; tel: 928 867 307; www.quiksilversurfschoolfuerteventura.com) provides courses at all levels, accommodation as well as surf safaris.

DIVING

For diving in **Lanzarote**'s three main resorts, contact Calipso Diving (c.c. Calipso Local 3, Avenida de las Islas Canarias, Costa Teguise; tel: 928 590 879; www.calipso-diving.com), which runs PADI/BSAC courses, plus family snorkelling excursions; Big Blue Sea Dive Center (Calle La Tegala 20, Costa Teguise; tel: 928 519 141; http://big-blue-sea.com/) for beginners' PADI courses and advanced courses, children's courses, scuba diving and wreck and cave diving; Manta Diving (Avenida Juan Carlos I 6, Local 5, Puerto del Carmen; tel: 928 516 815, mobile: 649 121 142; www.manta-diving-lanzarote.com), which offers PADI courses and daily dives and specialises in 'Discover Scuba' shallow-water dives and snorkelling for children. On Isla Graciosa dive courses are run by Buceo La Graciosa at the Archipélago Chinijo (tel: 928 842 213; www.buceolagraciosa.es).

Diving opportunities are numerous on **Fuerteventura**, especially in Corralejo. Abyss Divers (Pro Centre, Calle Gravina 8, Corralejo; tel: 928 949 004; www.abyssfuerteventura.com) is Irish-owned and has a good reputation. Dive Center Corralejo, (Nuestra Señora del Pino 22, Corralejo; tel: 928 535 906, mobile: 610 708 344 or 345; www.divecentercorralejo.com) takes divers to more than 40 sites, runs classes at all levels and has an indoor instruction pool. Punta Amanay Dive Center (Calle El Pulpo s/n, Edificio Dunas Club, Corralejo; tel: 928 535 357, mobile: 639 171 949; www.punta-amanay.com) runs dives in El Cotillo, El Jablito, Caleta de Fuste and Morro Jable. In the south there is Jandia Divers (Hotel Iberostar Palace, Pajara; tel: 928 540 444; www.jandiadivers.com).

SPORT FISHING

The biggest operator on **Lanzarote** runs boats from Puerto del Carmen and Puerto Calero marina (tel: 928 514 322, mobile: 629 731 29; www.sportfishinglanzarote.com), offering shark fishing, game fishing, bottom fishing and trawling on well-equipped boats. Transport to and from your hotel and lunch are included in all-day trips. It also does private charters. On **Fuerteventura**, there is fly-fishing and angling from *Barvik* on Corralejo's Muelle Deportivo (tel: 928 535 710) and *Pez Velero* (tel: 928 866 173).

SAILING

On **Lanzarote**, Endeavour Sailing (tel: 928 849 670; www.endeavour-sailing.co.uk), based in Puerto Calero, offers sailing courses and charters. Charter yachts with skippers can be hired from larger marinas at Arrecife, El Cable, Puerto Calero and Playa

Blanca. On **Fuerteventura**, Sail the Canaries (www.sailthecanaries.com) organises sailing courses and charters from its base in Corralejo.

BOAT TRIPS

Among many companies competing for business on **Lanzarote** are Líneas Marítimas Romero (Avenida Virgen del Mar, 119A, Isla Graciosa; tel: 928 842 055; www.lineasromero.com), with trips from Orzola to Isla Graciosa up to ten times a day in high summer, and Biosfera Express (www.biosferaexpress.com).

Princess Yaiza is a glass-bottomed boat that runs from Playa Blanca harbour and Marina Rubicón to Playa de Papagayo four times a day (tel: 928 514 322). Note that the boat can't go right to the beach so the last bit is done on a dinghy. Many boat trips can be pre-booked online and most companies will pick you up from or near your hotel.

From Marina Rubicón, Playa Blanca (tel: 928 519 012; www.marinarubicon.com), catamarans make trips to Playa Papagayo, with opportunities for jet-skiing and snorkelling. Submarine Safaris (Módulo C, Puerto Calero; tel: 928 512 898; www.submarinesafaris.com), makes trips beneath the sea in a yellow (naturally) submarine.

Most of **Fuerteventura**'s boat trips tend to be in the north of the island, where the winds and waves are not as strong as

Kicking up dust on a jeep safari

in the south. Catlanza (Puerto de Corralejo; tel: 928 513 022, mobile: 638 454 539; www.catlanza.com) organises catamaran trips to Lanzarote's Papagayo beaches, and also does corporate and private charters. Excursiones Marítimas (Corralejo; tel: 699 687 294; www.excursionesmaritimaslobos.com) run several no-frills trips a day to the Isla de Lobos on *El Majorero*, *Isla de Lobos* and *Celia Cruz*; buy tickets at the harbour kiosks.

JEEP AND QUAD BIKE SAFARIS

On **Lanzarote** there are various jeep and quad bike safaris organised by Adventure Holidays Lanzarote (tel: 649 389 888; www.adventureholidayslanzarote.com) and Touristticket (Puerto del Carmen; tel: 629 731 293; http://touristticket.com).

In **Fuerteventura** Discovery Safari (tel: 928 775 188; http://discoverysafari.es), runs jeep tours all over the island. Fuerte Trike (tel: 928 875 630; www.fuerte-trike.com) organises quad bike tours from various starting points. Quad Adventure (tel: 928 866 552; http://new.quadadventure.net) organises quad and buggy expeditions as well as safaris from its base on Playa Blanca.

BIKE HIRE AND TOURS

Road and mountain bikes are available for hire in all the resorts. On **Lanzarote** try Bike Station (Centro Comercial Las Maretas, Avenida Isla de las Canarias, Costa Teguise; tel: 628 102 177; www.mylanzarote.com). In Playa Blanca go to Electro Bike (Centro Comercial Punta Limones; tel: 652 200 570; www.electro bike-lanzarote.com). In Puerto del Carmen there's Renner Bike (Avenida de las Playas, Centro Comercial Marítimo 25; tel: 928 510 612; www.mountainbike-lanzarote.com).

Fuerteventura has Easy Riders (Calle Las Dunas s/n, Corralejo; tel: 637 408 233; www.easyriders-bikecenter.com) for mountain- and road-bike tours of the north of the island, while Backtrax (Hotel Elba Castillo, Caleta de Fuste; tel: 656 753 055; www.backtrax1.com) does off-road motorbike tours and Caleta Cycles (Caleta de Fuste; tel: 676 600 190; www.caletacycles.com) rents bikes and organises tours at various levels. Lanzarote Cycling (Calle Timanfaya 8 Local 4, Puerto del Carmen; tel: 654 152 579; www.lanzarote-cycling.com) offers MTB and road bike tours.

HIKING

On **Lanzarote** Canary Trekking (Calle La Laguna 8, Costa Teguise; tel: 609 537 684/696 900 929; www.canarytrekking.com) conducts guided walks in Timanfaya National

Be prepared

Bike and buggy hire and excursions include insurance (check whether it is third-party or comprehensive) and provide helmets, but you must bring your driving licence and a credit card to act as a deposit.

Park, the Playa de Famara Natural Park, and the protected land-scape of La Geria. Windsurfing Club Las Cucharas (see page 81) also offers guided walks through volcanic landscapes. On **Fuerteventura** Caminatas Hiking, (Villa Volcana, Calle la Berlina 11, Villaverde; tel: 928 868 690) organises a variety of treks on a network of hiking trails.

HORSE AND CAMEL RIDING

Lanzarote a Caballo (Carretera Arrecife–Yaiza, Km 17, Yaiza; tel: 928 830 038; www.lanzaroteacaballo.com) offers treks of varying lengths for beginners and experienced riders. Camel rides and buggy tours are also available.

GOLF

On **Lanzarote** Costa Teguise Golf Club (Avenida del Golf s/n, Costa Teguise; tel: 928 590 512; www.lanzarote-golf.com) is an

18-hole course open to non-members that also offers lessons. You can also play at Lanzarote Golf (www.lanzarotegolfresort. com). On **Fuerteventura** there's the Fuerteventura Golf Resort (Carretera de Jandía, Km 11, Caleta de Fuste; tel: 928 160 005; www.fuerteventuragolfresort.com). Other golf clubs include Golf Club Salinas de Antigua (www.salinasgolf.com), Las Playitas Golf (www.playitas.info) and Jandia Golf (www.jandiagolf.com).

CHILDREN'S ACTIVITIES

There's lots for children to do on both islands, as well as play on the beach. Taking them out in the evening isn't a problem, either, as most restaurants welcome children. Many hotel complexes have entertainment geared to children between three and 10 years old. Most children, except the very young, will also enjoy the boat and submarine trips listed above and other excursions, such as the bus tour around the Ruta de Volcanos (see page 55).

WATER PARKS

There is at least one on each island. On **Lanzarote** it is Aquapark (Avenida de Teguise, Costa Teguise; tel: 928 592 128; http://aqua parklanzarote.es; daily 10am–6pm), with all the usual pools, chutes, slides and activities. On **Fuerteventura** there is Acua Water Park (Avenida Nuestra Señora del Carmen 41, Corralejo; tel: 928 537 034; www.acuawaterpark.com; daily 10am–5.30pm) for all kinds of watery fun.

GO-KARTING

Gran Karting Club (Carretera Arrecife–Tias Km 7, 2km/1.2 miles from Lanzarote airport; tel: 928 524 926; http://grankartingclub lanzarote.com/es/) offers karts and tracks for children and adults, and even 'mini motos' for the under-fives.

ANIMAL ATTRACTIONS

One of **Lanzarote**'s best-known attractions is the Echadero de Camellos in Parque Nacional de Timanfaya (daily 9am–5pm), where children and adults alike find it hard to resist the camel rides. Lanzarote a Caballo (http://lanzaroteacaballo.com; see page 88) is a good riding school for adults and children; they also do paintball sessions. Las Pardelas (Orzola; tel: 928 842 545; www.pardelas-park.com; daily 10am–6pm) is a family-run place with donkey rides and a playground. Rancho Texas (Puerto del Carmen; tel: 928 516 897; https://ranchotexaslanzarote.com; daily 9.30am–5.30pm; free transport from resort hotels) puts on several shows a day; there are crocodiles, parrots and birds of prey, canoes and pony rides.

One of **Fuerteventura**'s big draws is Oceanarium Explorer (daily 10am–6pm; http://oceanariumexplorer.com), Puerto Castillo Yacht Harbour (Caleta de Fuste; tel: 928 547 687) with a glass-bottomed, non-diving submarine and a catamaran for dolphin-spotting trips. Also popular is Oasis Park Fuerteventura (Carretera General de Jandía, La Lajita; tel: 928 161 102; www.fuerteventuraoasispark.com; daily 9am–6pm), with camel rides, giraffes, reptiles, sea lions, parrots and birds of prey.

SHOPPING

Shopping is not a major activity on either island, but there are some interesting items. Among them are consumables: *mojo* sauce can be bought in small jars in many places, as can cactus honey, wine from La Geria and the ubiquitous rum-and-honey liqueur called Ronmiel. Majorero cheese, made in Fuerteventura, can also be bought on both islands.

Aloe vera products of all kinds can be found everywhere. There are some specialist shops and stalls in markets, but

The reptile show at Fuerteventura's La Lajita Oasis Park

products are also available in souvenir shops and supermarkets. Lanzaloe (www.lanzaloe.com) is an ecologically aware organisation based in Orzola that supplies large quantities of aloe vera to pharmaceutical and cosmetics companies. Other items include ceramics – nothing startlingly original, but you can find some good modern copies of traditional pottery – and peridot jewellery (see page 58). There is also hand-embroidered table linen and basketwork. The genuine articles are usually found in artisans' centres or museums; because it is such labour-intensive work, they are quite expensive.

Some places on **Lanzarote** worth checking out for comestibles are: Ahumaderia de Uga (Ctra Arrecife–Yaiza, Uga) for excellent smoked salmon; Territorio Sibarita (Calle Otilia Diaz 14, Arrecife) and MisQuesitos (Calle León y Castillo 58) which both have a good selection of delicatessen items – cheese, ham, *mojo* sauces and honey, as well as local wine; and the Bodega

Traditional-style ceramics

El Grifo (www.elgrifo.com) and Bodega Barreto (http://www.vinosdetegueste.com/bodega-barreto), next door to each other on the main road at La Florida, which both sell their own wine. The white *malvasía* is best, whether you like it sweet, dry or medium. You can taste before you buy.

For craftwork, there is the Taller de Artesanía (Plaza de León y Castillo, Haría) a co-operative that sells pottery, basket work and embroidered items, which can also be found in Haría's Saturday market. At the Centro de Artesanía at the Monumento del Campesino in Mozaga you can buy traditional-style items made on the premises, as well as wine from nearby La Geria.

The Fundación César Manrique in Tahiche has a good selection of items with the artist's designs, ranging from prints and ceramics to canvas bags, scarves and aprons – all very well-priced. The Fundación also has outlets in Teguise and in Puerto del Carmen (next to the tourist office).

Teguise market is the best-known and biggest on Lanzarote, but most of the goods are not local – a lot of them are made in the Far East. However, there are a number of shops in the town that are open on Sunday and sell better-quality stuff. These include: Galería de Arte Ángel Cabrera (Calle Reyes Católicos), with a good selection of watercolours, ceramics and silks, and Bazar Artesanía (Plaza San Francisco 4), which sells *timples* (five-string guitars typical of Lanzarote) and traditional sun hats, alongside other items. Aloe Plus (Plaza de la Constitución 4) specialises in aloe vera and beauty products.

On **Fuerteventura** Majorero cheese is one of the best buys. Hijos de Vera Montelongo (Calle de la Casa Alta 15, Tindaya) is one of the island's best-known cheese makers, and sells direct from its production centre and from La Casa de Ganadero (Calle Salamanca 12, Puerto del Rosario), which also sells other island produce.

Craftwork on Fuerteventura can be found in the Casa Santa María Centro de Artesanía (www.casasantamaria.net) in Betancuria. Traditional woven and embroidered items and pottery are sold in the museum shop, along with *mojo* sauce, cactus honey, wine and liqueurs. At the Escuela de Artesanía Canaria (Plaza Santa María, Lajares) you can see women embroidering table linen by hand, and buy the products.

The best range of contemporary posters, prints and ceramics (along with those at the Fundación César Manrique) can be found at the Centro de Arte Canario (Casa Mané, La Oliva; www.centrodeartecanario.com) and they are very reasonably priced.

NIGHTLIFE AND FESTIVALS

Most of the islands' nightlife is provided either in the resort hotels, which usually have middle-of-the-road live acts several times a week, or in the bars and discos of the commercial centres, which tend to have quite a high turnover rate. Temporary structures are often set up on or near the beaches for performances by rock and pop groups. Corralejo and El Cotillo, on Fuerteventura, have the best reputation for rock, pop and jazz – posters and flyers in the resorts will tell you what's on where. Corralejo's best-known live music venue is the Rock Island

Making music in Corralejo

Bar (www.rockislandbar.com). El Almacén (Calle Betancort, Arrecife) often has jazz, rock or guitar music on Friday nights (the Cabildo puts out a monthly leaflet, called *Cultura*, listing events here and in the theatres in San Bartolomé and Teguise). The centre also has a small cinema which shows art-house films, but these are all in Spanish, as are those in Arrecife's mainstream cinema (Multicines Atlántida, Charco de San Ginés).

In October, the Visual Music Festival of Lanzarote (https://festivaldemusicavisualdelanzarote.com/en) stages performances of contemporary music in interesting venues all over the island – chiefly the auditoriums in the Cueva de los Verdes and the Jameos del Agua, as well as the Convento de Santo Domingo in Teguise.

There is one casino, Gran Casino de Lanzarote (Avenida de las Playas 12, Puerto del Carmen; tel: 928 515 000; www.grancasinolanzarote.com; daily 10pm–4am, restaurant 8pm–2am; dress smartly and take your passport).

CALENDAR OF EVENTS

6 January Cabalgata de Reyes (Procession of the Three Kings), Arrecife. The kings parade through the streets on camels, throwing sweets to children. Some processions in other towns on both islands.

February–early March Carnival. Celebrations, held in most towns and resorts on both islands, staggered so they do not clash with each other. Several days of flamboyant fun start with the *murgas*, a parade of costumed revellers accompanied by whistles and drums. Carnival ends with the *entierro de la sardina*, a strange ritual common to all Spanish carnival celebrations, in which a papier-mâché model of a sardine is burnt.

Late March–mid-April Semana Santa. The week preceeding Easter is a time of solemn processions.

Mid-June Corpus Christi. Intricately designed carpets of salt, dyed various colours, cover the roads around the Iglesia de San Ginés in Arrecife, where processions are held.

23 June San Juan. On the eve of the saint's day bonfires are lit in some town and village squares. The biggest celebration is in Haría.

14 July San Buenaventura. The island's patron saint is celebrated throughout Fuerteventura but especially in Betancuria.

16 July Nuestra Señora del Carmen. The patron saint of fishermen and sailors is celebrated in most coastal places with street processions and decorated boats. Biggest celebrations on Lanzarote are in Puerto del Carmen, Playa Blanca, Isla Graciosa and, although it is inland, Teguise. On Fuerteventura, Morro Jable and Corralejo stage the most colourful events.

25 August San Ginés celebrations. Festivities in honour of Arrecife's patron saint include processions and dancing; they last about a week.

Early September Nuestra Señora de los Volcanes. According to legend, the Virgin halted the flow of lava from a volcanic eruption in 1824 and saved the village of Mancha Blanca, Lanzarote. She is honoured with a pilgrimage, a folklore festival, an artisans' fair and bouts of *lucha canaria*. Gran Tarajal, Fuerteventura: Open International Fishing Competition.

Mid-November Kite Festival: Playa del Burro, Corralejo. Kite-flyers from all over the world come to this two-day event.

EATING OUT

Canary Islands food has much in common with that of mainland Spain, but with some interesting regional differences. There are also dishes similar to those found in parts of Latin America – although whether these recipes were introduced to the New World by Canarian emigrants, or American inventions brought back by returnees, is debatable.

You will also find restaurants where the cooking is described as *cocina vasca* (Basque), because a number of cooks from this northern region of Spain have come to work on the island or opened their own restaurants here. Their familiarity with Atlantic fish and seafood is a considerable bonus given the abundant local supply and the Basque region has a reputation for some of the best cooking in Spain.

WHERE AND WHEN TO EAT

When it comes to places to eat, the choices are between the fish restaurants that line the seafronts and harbours; the places serving typically Canarian food, which are found mainly in the towns and villages – although there are a few in the resorts; and the all-purpose pizza, pasta and burger joints. There are a few expensive venues, but most are very reasonably priced. You may see restaurants advertising *cocina casalinga* or *comidas caseras* – this simply means home cooking, and, while the quality may vary, it is a sign that you will be getting authentic, and inexpensive, island food. There are not many places that style themselves tapas bars, but in many middle-of-the-range and inexpensive restaurants there will be a variety of tapas on offer, and some of the portions are quite large – two or three would make a meal for most people. You

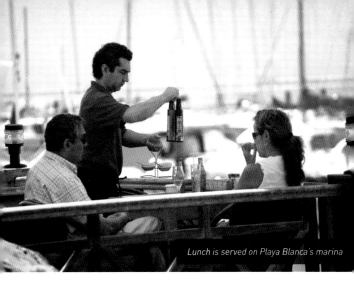
Lunch is served on Playa Blanca's marina

will also see *raciones* (portions) advertised: these are larger than tapas, but not full meals.

Bars are generally places in which to drink, not eat, although many will serve sandwiches *(bocadillos)* or a limited range of tapas. A *piscolabis* is a bar serving a variety of little sandwiches and snacks. (See page 111 for a selection of recommended restaurants.)

The islanders, like the people of mainland Spain, eat late. Between two and three o'clock is the time to sit down to lunch, and ten o'clock is not too late for dinner. Some restaurants may close between lunch and dinner, but many serve food all day. Those that cater mostly to foreign visitors, aware that habits are different, will have their lunch menus out by midday and serve dinner as early as you like.

Sunday lunch is a major event, and as this continues throughout the afternoon many restaurants are closed on

Sunday evening. Some also close one evening during the week, and a number of places will close for a month in early summer to prepare themselves for their busy season in July and August.

FISH

The waters around the islands are rich in fish, which turn up on menus in the restaurants. Along with the ubiquitous *sardinas*, fresh from the ocean, the fish most commonly seen on menus are *corvina* (a kind of sea bass), *cherne* (wreckfish or stone bass), *sama* (sea bream) and *bacalao* (salt cod). You will also find *merluza* (hake), *atún* (tuna) and seafood such as *gambas* (prawns), *pulpo* (octopus), *calamares* (squid) and *almejas* (clams).

Fish will often be served simply grilled along with salad, *mojo* sauce and *papas arrugadas* (see page 101), but there are numerous other ways that it may appear on your table. *Sancocho canario* is a popular dish, a stew made with red grouper or sea bass, potatoes and yams, spiced up with a hot variety of *mojo* sauce. *Salpicón de pescado* is another dish you may see on menus; this is sea bass cooked, chopped and served cold with a mixture of onions, garlic, tomatoes and peppers, topped with hard boiled egg and olives. A delicacy introduced from the Basque country is *calamares rellenos de bacalao* – small squid with a cod-based stuffing, sometimes served in a creamy sauce (a similar dish is made with stuffed peppers – *pimientos*).

Authentic offerings

In the resorts, you may have to bypass numerous restaurants offering burgers, chips, pasta and pizza, not to mention all-day English breakfasts, before you find ones serving genuinely Canarian – or even Spanish – food, but they do exist. And good fresh fish, simply cooked, can be found almost everywhere.

Fresh grilled fish

Paella is not a Canary Island dish, but you can still find it, along with other rice and seafood dishes such as *arroz negra* (rice with squid and squid ink, which makes it black).

MEAT

If you don't like fish, don't despair – there's plenty of meat to be found. *Cabrito* (kid) and *conejo* (rabbit) are most common, but pork *(cerdo)* and chicken *(pollo)* are popular, and there are some good steaks to be had as well. Goat and rabbit are often served *al salmorejo* (with green peppers, in a herb and garlic marinade). Chorizo – the red spicy sausage found all over Spain – also crops up in a variety of guises.

SOUPS

Most of the world's traditional dishes originated as a way of filling stomachs with what was available and inexpensive. In the Canary Islands, this meant a whole range of substantial soups and stews. *Ropa vieja* (literally, old clothes) may not sound very appetising, but it's a tasty mixture of meat, tomatoes and chickpeas; *puchero* includes meat, pumpkin and any vegetables available; while *rancho canario*, made with chicken, chorizo, bacon, chickpeas and various herbs, is the most elaborate and, some say, the best.

Vegetarians should be aware that even such innocent-sounding dishes as watercress soup *(potaje de berros)*, a staple found on many menus, has chunks of bacon in it, and celery soup *(potaje de apio)* may contain scraps of pork.

VEGETABLES

The vegetables you are offered will be those that are in season, and, because the island does not produce a great variety

---

☉ CHEESE

Fuerteventura is known for its goat's cheese, Majorero, which has been awarded a *denominación de origen controlada* (DOC) and is said to be one of the best of its kind in Spain. Goat's milk – which must be unpasteurised to make the cheese – has a high fat content and is very aromatic. The young, fresh cheese has a white rind and a crumbly texture; the matured version has a yellow rind, which may be rubbed with oil or paprika or, sometimes, *gofio*. You will find it on most menus in Fuerteventura, and quite a few on Lanzarote. You will also see cheeses from Gran Canaria: *queso de flor*, a soft cheese that is a mixture of sheep's and cow's milk curdled with the juice of flowers from the cardoon thistle; and *queso tierno de Valsequillo*, which ranges in flavour from mild to strong – the stronger it is the darker the colour.

and imports are expensive, choice may be limited. Pulses such as lentils (*lentejas*) and chickpeas (*garbanzos*) are used a lot. Canary tomatoes are delicious – although most of those you get here will have been imported from Gran Canaria – and Lanzarote onions are far sweeter than those from mainland Spain. If you like garlic, ask for *tomates aliñados*, tomato salad smothered with olive oil and garlic. *Pimientos de padrón* – small green peppers cooked whole and covered with salt – originated in Galicia and are now found everywhere. Avocados (strictly speaking a fruit, not a vegetable) are served at a perfect stage of ripeness.

Mojo rojo and mojo verde

Most dishes contain or are accompanied by potatoes (*papas*). You won't go far without encountering *papas arrugadas* (wrinkled potatoes), which are served with meat and fish or by themselves as tapas. They are small potatoes – the yellow-fleshed Tenerife variety are best – cooked in their skins in salted water, then left to dry over a low heat until their skins wrinkle and a salty crust forms. It is said that this dish originated with fishermen who used to boil the potatoes in sea water.

MOJO

Papas arrugadas, and many meat dishes, are usually accompanied by *mojo rojo*, a sauce whose basic ingredients are tomatoes, peppers and paprika. A spicier version *(mojo picón)* contains hot chilli pepper as well. *Mojo verde* is a green sauce made with oil, vinegar, garlic, coriander and/or parsley, usually served with fish. The sauces arrive at the table in small bowls, so you can use as much or as little as you like. Every restaurant – and probably every home – seems to have their own version, and entire *mojo* recipe books are published.

GOFIO

Made of wheat, barley or a mixture of the two, *gofio* was the staple food of the Guanches and still forms an essential part of the diet today. The cereal is toasted before being ground into flour, and then has a multiplicity of uses. It is stirred into soups and into children's milk, used to thicken sauces, and mixed with oil, salt and sugar into a kind of bread, not unlike polenta. It is also blended with fish stock to make a thick soup called *gofio escaldado*.

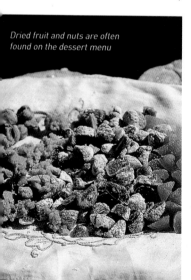

Dried fruit and nuts are often found on the dessert menu

FRUIT AND DESSERTS

There is not enough rain to grow much fruit in Lanzarote or Fuerteventura, but products imported from mainland Spain or the other islands are usually delicious when in season. On many menus desserts are limited to ice cream (*helado*), flan (the ubiquitous caramel custard), fresh fruit, dried fruit and nuts, and the one you see everywhere, *bienmesabe*, which translates as 'tastes good to me' – and so it does. There are numerous recipes, but basically it is a mixture of crushed almonds, lemon, sugar (lots), cinnamon and egg yolks.

WHAT TO DRINK

The breakfast drink is coffee. *Café solo* is a small, strong black, like an espresso; a *cortado*, served in a glass, is a shot of coffee with a small amount of hot milk; *café con leche* is a large milky coffee. An *Americano* is a shot of coffee with added hot water. However, espresso and cappuccino are widely understood terms. Hot chocolate is sometimes available for breakfast, but if you ask for tea you will just get a teabag in a little pot.

You are advised not to drink tap water, but *agua mineral* is available everywhere – *con gas* is sparkling, *sin gas* is still. *Zumo de naranja*, freshly squeezed orange juice, is widely available, and in some bars you can get more exotic juices.

Wine is usually drunk with meals, most of it imported from the mainland; Rioja is one of the favourites. But Lanzarote does produce its own wine: *malvasía*, known in English as malmsey. Shakespeare alluded to malmsey several times, and the duke of Clarence drowned in a vat of it in 1478. Although this is best known as a sweet wine, there are excellent dry and semi-dry varieties, and some reds, although the whites are better. The grapes are grown in the volcanic soil of the La Geria region, where you can visit bodegas, and in the far north of the island, near the Mirador del Río. El Grifo is regarded as the best, but Barreto is also a reputable producer. You will

Restaurants with terraces by the sea are always popular

find local wines in many restaurants, usually quite reasonably priced. Neighbouring Gran Canaria has some 32 wineries, and a recently introduced *denominación de origen controlada* (DOC); Monte Lentiscal, which has its own DOC, is one to look out for. Tenerife is a bigger producer, but its wines are not regularly found in restaurants.

Rum, some of which is produced at Arucas, Gran Canaria, forms the basis of Ronmiel, in which the spirit is blended with honey and lemon in a pleasant, sweet liqueur. You may also find Guindilla, a cherry liqueur from Gran Canaria, and Manzana Verde, an apple-based schnapps that is actually made in Cataluña but is widely available here.

Beer is extremely popular. You will see familiar Spanish brands such as San Miguel, and imported German and English beers, along with the Canary Islands' own Tropical and Dorada. If you want a draught beer, ask for a *caña*.

TO HELP YOU ORDER

Could we have a table? **¿Nos puede dar una mesa?**
Do you have a set menu? **¿Tiene un menú del día?**
I'd like... **Quisiera...**

beer **una cerveza**
bread **pan**
coffee **un café**
dessert **un postre**
fish **pescado**
fruit **fruta**
glass **un vaso**
ice cream **un helado**
meat **carne**
menu **la carta**

milk **leche**
mineral water **agua mineral**
potatoes **patatas/papas**
rice **arroz**
salad **una ensalada**
sandwich **un bocadillo**
sugar **azúcar**
tea **un té**
wine **vino**

MENU READER

aceitunas olives
albóndigas meatballs
almejas baby clams
anchoas anchovies
atún tuna
bacalao cod
besugo sea bream
boquerones fresh anchovies
calamares squid
caracoles snails
cerdo pork
chuletas chops
cocido stew
cordero lamb
entremeses hors-d'oeuvres
gambas prawns

langosta spiny lobster
langostino large prawn
mariscos shellfish
mejillones mussels
melocotón peach
navajas razor clams
ostras oysters
pastel cake
pollo chicken
pulpitos baby octopus
salsa sauce
sepia cuttlefish
ternera veal
tortilla omelette
trucha trout
uvas grapes

PLACES TO EAT

We have used the following symbols to give an idea of the price for a three-course meal for one, including house wine, cover and service:

€€€   45–65 euros
€€   35–45 euros
€   below 35 euros

LANZAROTE: ARRECIFE

Bodegón los Conejeros €–€€ *Avenida Rafael González Negrin 9, tel: 928 817 195.* Some great Canarian tapas are served in this unassuming wood-beamed bodega. Smoking permitted throughout. Dinner only. Reservations advised, especially on Friday and Saturday night. Closed Sun.

QuéMUAC €€ *Castillo de San José, Arrecife, tel: 928 812 321.* This restaurant in the Castillo de San José, which also houses the Museo Internacional de Arte Contemporáneo, offers a great selection of tapas and some tasty fish and meat dishes based on local products, plus sweeping vistas over the sea. Closed Sun–Mon.

La Puntilla €€ *Avenida César Manrique 51, tel: 928 816 042,* http://lapuntillacomidas.es. Overlooking the Charco, La Puntilla is an attractive place that serves excellent fish – what's on offer depends on what's been caught that day. They are also well known for their rice dishes, and there is always meat on the menu. Smoking area. Closed Sun.

Mediterranean Altamar €€–€€€ *Arrecife Gran Hotel, Parque Islas Canarias, tel: 928 800 000,* www.aghotelspa.com. On the 17th floor of the island's only high-rise building (see page 29). The international-style food is well cooked and well presented in a somewhat formal atmosphere. The views are great. Daily dinner only.

NORTHERN LANZAROTE
Arrieta

El Amanecer €€ *Calle La Garita 44, Playa Honda, tel: 928 848 390, no bookings*. A popular and highly recommended harbour-side fish restaurant, open Fri–Wed 10am–8pm. Arrive before 1pm for lunch if you want to avoid queuing for a table.

El Charcón €–€€ *Muelle de Arrieta, tel: 928 848 110*. An attractive little place, right by the quay, with lots of outside tables. Reliably good fish dishes. Closed Wed.

Haría

Dos Hermanos €€ *Plaza León y Castillo, tel: 928 835 409*, http://restaurante doshermanos.es. In the middle of town, this busy place serves Canarian specialities such as goat *(cabra)* and rabbit *(conejo)*, as well as seafood. Always busy at Sunday lunch time. Open daily 9am–8pm.

El Cortijo €€ *Calle El Palmeral 6, tel: 928 835 686*, http://elcortijodeharia. blogspot.com. Canarian country food, including rabbit dishes, are served in an attractive whitewashed building. Open Tue–Sun 9am–5pm.

Restaurant Mirador de los Valles €–€€ *Los Valles (LZ10 between Teguise and Haría), tel: 928 52 81 14*. Local dishes and stunning views at this mirador restaurant. Open daily noon–8pm.

Orzola

Pardelas Park €–€€ *Calle la Quemadita 88, tel: 928 842 545*, www.pardelas-park.com. Unpretentious, reasonably priced restaurant located in the Pardelas Park. Try their seafood dishes. Open daily 10am–7pm.

Punta Fariones €€ *Calle de la Quemadita 10, tel: 928 84 25 26*. Harbour-side restaurant; fish is the speciality, but there are meat dishes as well, mostly grilled, some with *mojo* sauces. Open Wed–Mon 10am–6pm.

CENTRAL LANZAROTE

Costa Teguise

El Navarro €€ *Avenida del Mar 13, tel: 928 592 145*. A bit hard to find, as it's at the southwest end of the town in the Santa Rosa area, but worth it. Steaks and seafood are equally good and the puddings delight those who love puddings. Booking advisable. Closed Sun.

El Patio €€ *Plaza del Pueblo Marinero, tel: 928 591 102,* www.patiolanzarote.com. Italian restaurant that does a good carpaccio of salmon and interesting meat dishes. Also a full range of pizzas (from a wood-fired oven) and pastas which puts it in the € bracket. Open daily noon–midnight.

Restaurante Grill La Vaca Loca €€, *Avenida de las Islas Canarias 2, tel: 928 94 54 18*. Juicy Argentinian steaks prepared over a hot flame are arguably the best in town as is the garlic prawn starter. Good Rioja wines and Sangria. Friendly staff. Open Wed–Mon 1–10.30pm.

Patio Canario €–€€ *Pueblo Marinero, tel: 928 346 234,* www.patiocanariolanzarote.com. One of the few places in this resort serving genuine Canarian food. There's a wide selection, including *pimientos rellenos de bacalao* (small peppers stuffed with cod, in a creamy sauce). Has a large, wood-panelled dining room and tables outside in a quiet, shady square. Friendly, helpful staff.

Mozaga/San Bartolomé

Caserio de Mozaga €€–€€€ *Mozaga, tel: 657 640 514,* http://caseriodemozaga.com. The restaurant in this casa rural is known as one of the best places to eat on the island (no lunch). Excellent fresh ingredients and some wonderful puddings served in the attractive setting of a converted barn. Booking is essential.

Centro de Artesanía €€ *Monumento al Campesino, San Bartolomé, tel: 928 517 760*. Authentic Canarian food: *ropa vieja* (meat, tomatoes and chickpeas), *cabra* (goat) and *conejo* (rabbit) as well as fish, in this intriguing place. You can have tapas at the bar or at outside tables, or sit in the huge, palm-decked, domed restaurant for a full meal. Lunch only.

Puerto del Carmen

El Sardinero € *Corner of Calle Nuestra Señora del Carmen and Avenida del Varadero, tel: 928 515 234.* This cosy little fish restaurant overlooking the harbour is highly regarded by local people and usually busy.

La Lonja €€–€€€ *Plaza El Varadero s/n, tel: 928 511 377.* This is the place to eat fish. A large, two-storey dining room and a long wooden counter displaying tempting dishes. No outside tables, but it's right by the harbour, and they have their own excellent fish shop next door. Does a great *parillada de mariscos* (grilled mixed seafood). Open daily 7am–midnight.

La Ola €€–€€€ *Avenida de las Playas 35, tel: 928 515 500,* www.cafelaola. com. La Ola is a part of the Lani chain that has a number of restaurants on the island. Upstairs there are comfy white sofas and sunbeds set around a small pool with a great view of the sea; downstairs, vivid, silky cushions and low tables. The menu features mostly rice dishes, meat and fresh fish. Open daily 10am–2am.

Puerto Bahía €€–€€€ *Avenida del Varadero 5, tel: 928 513 793.* Another harbour-side restaurant with excellent seafood, but good grilled meats and some vegetarian dishes as well. Obliging staff and lovely views. Open daily 10am–midnight.

Vino + Lanzarote € *Calle Barracuda, local 14, tel: 928 516 959.* Small, cozy wine bar with friendly staff, a good choice of tapas and delicious desserts. Excellent value. Helpful owner and staff. Open Mon–Sat noon–1am.

Teguise

Ikarus Gastro Art €€ *Clavijo y Fajardo 6, tel: 928 84 57 01.* Cosy, red-walled rooms, with a great chef behind the scenes. The sophisticated menu includes excellent grilled lamb and the duck breast in balsamic sauce is not to be missed. The desserts are superb too. Closed Mon.

La Cantina €–€€ *Calle León y Castillo 8, tel: 928 845 536,* http://cantina teguise.com. A series of small rooms and a patio to choose from in this old Canarian house. There are various kinds of 'sharing platters' – although that doesn't extend to the popular chocolate brownies. Friendly owners and pleasant atmosphere. Very busy at Sunday lunch time. Open 10am–11pm.

Restaurante Hesperides €€ *Calle León y Castillo 3, tel: 928 59 48 64,* http://restaurantehesperides.blogspot.com. This is a nice restaurant with tasteful decor, set in a traditional Canarian house. The dishes are well-presented and cooked to perfection, and the staff attentive.

SOUTHERN LANZAROTE

El Golfo

El Golfo €–€€ *Avenida Marítima 98, tel: 928 173 147.* Dining areas upstairs and down, inside and out. Good paella and other rice dishes, including *arroz negra* (black rice).

Mar Azul €–€€ *Avenida del Golfo 42, tel: 928 173 132,* www.mar-azul.es. This is a pretty blue-and-white restaurant with tables set right by the sea. It specialises, naturally, in seafood, fresh from the sea and prepared with care. Open daily 10am–9.30pm.

Macher

La Cabaña €€€ *LZ2 Carretera Arrecife–Uga, tel: 650 685 662,* www.laca banamacher.com. Excellent restaurant run by an English husband-and-wife team. There is more meat than fish; steak with black truffles and chestnut mushrooms is one of the signature dishes. Open Tuesday to Saturday from 7pm. Reservations essential.

La Tegala €€€ *LZ2 Carretera Tías–Yaiza 60, tel: 928 524 524,* www.lategala. com. In a striking building – modern and glass-walled yet somehow attuned to the surrounding countryside. Delicious Canarian dishes with an innovative touch. Closed Sun.

Playa Blanca

Brisa Marina €€ *Avenida Marítima 97–98, tel: 928 517 206,* www.restaurante
brisamarina.com. Large, green-shuttered seafront restaurant. Lots of fish,
simply grilled with *mojo* sauces and a variety of rice dishes *(arroces)*.

Blue Note Lanzarote €€ *Marina Rubicon 12/b, tel: 928 519 634.* Jazz bar
and restaurant in one, right by the sea. The burgers are delicious and
the fish is fresh. The friendly staff supply blankets when it gets chilly and
there is great live music. Open 24hrs.

L'Artista €€ *Calle La Tegala 18–20, tel: 928 517 578.* Just one street back
from the beach, but with sea views, this attractive, green-balconied
restaurant serves good Italian food, from *mare e monti* to pizzas and
tiramisú. There's a good ambience, too. Open daily 1pm–midnight.

Yaiza/Timanfaya

El Diablo €€ *Parque Nacional de Timanfaya, tel: 928 840 057.* Meat is
barbecued over natural heat from the volcano in a large, Manrique-
designed restaurant with wrap-around views.

La Casona €€€ *Calle El Rincón 11, Yaiza, tel: 928 836 262,* www.casona
deyaiza.com. This attractive restaurant is set in an old winery in a casa
rural, but is open to non-residents. It specialises in dishes made, as far
as possible, from fresh, local ingredients.

La Era €€–€€€ *Trasera del Ayuntamiento, Yaiza, tel: 928 830 016,*
www.laera.com. This well-known restaurant serves outstanding island food in a 300-year-old Canarian farmhouse with a whitewashed
courtyard. An art-filled, wooden-beamed bar serves snacks and light
meals. Yet another César Manrique creation. Open daily noon–11pm.

FUERTEVENTURA: PUERTO DEL ROSARIO

Casa Toño €€ *Calle Alcalde Alonso Patallo 8, tel: 928 344 736.* The speciality is the Spanish kitchen, all the tapas dishes are really tasty and

servings are generous. The fresh tuna with pickled ginger is incredible. The menu is only in Spanish, but the staff are happy to help you choose. Closed Sun.

Trattoria da Sandro €€ *Calle Duero 23, tel: 928 852 567*, www.trattoria da-sandro.com. Long-established, typical Italian trattoria with a large choice of pasta dishes, salads, meats and, of course, pizzas – arguably the best on the island. The owners, Lena and Sandro are very helpful. Closed Wed.

NORTHERN FUERTEVENTURA

Corralejo

Cofradía de Pescadores €€ *Avenida Maritima 20, tel: 928 867 773*. Excellent fish, as you would expect at the fishermen's co-operative. *Lubina* (bass) baked in salt may be on the menu. Open daily 11am–11.30pm.

Ugly Duckling €€ *Calle Abubilla, tel: 618 04 48 96*. Very unexpected little place serving modern Scandinavian and Danish fare in a modern setting with a terrace. A glass of cava to start with is a nice touch and the service is excellent. Homemade chips and steaks prepared to perfection. The desserts are delicious and big enough to share. Closed Wed–Thu.

La Marquesina €€ *Calle El Muelle Chico, tel: 928 535 434*, www.restaurante lamarquesina.com. By the fisherman's statue on the harbour, this friendly restaurant is always busy with customers enjoying the fresh fish. Open daily 11am–midnight.

El Cotillo

Punta Dell'Est €€ *Calle Hermanas del Castillo 4, El Cotillo, tel: 928 538 483*. A popular Italian restaurant with mountain views and friendly staff. The seafood pasta, homemade bread and coffee are all excellent. Lunch and dinner. Closed Thu.

CENTRAL FUERTEVENTURA
Betancuria/Pájara

Casa Isaítas € *Calle Guize 7, Pájara, tel: 928 161 482, www.casaisaitas. com.* This pretty little hostel uses mostly local seasonal produce, which means there are lots of vegetables, hams and cheeses, but also meat and some fish dishes.

Casa Princess Arminda €–€€ *Calle Juan de Betancort 2, Betancuria, tel: 928 878 979.* This bar and restaurant in a house restored by the family who have owned it for 500 years – it's said to be one of the oldest on the island. Shaded bar, dining room and pretty courtyard, serving locally produced meat dishes as well as some fish and good puddings. Excellent goat stew.

Casa Santa María €€ *Plaza Santa María, Betancuria, tel: 928 878 282, www.casasantamaria.net.* In a lovingly restored 16th-century farmhouse close to the church, you can eat roast lamb *(cordero asado)*, kid *(cabrito)* and much more besides. There is also a cafeteria, serving tapas and light meals, on the other side of the road. Closed Sun.

Don Antonio €€€ *Plaza de la Peña, La Vega del Río de las Palmas (Betancuria), tel: 928 878 757.* One of the best restaurants on the island, serving original dishes made with locally sourced ingredients in a 17th-century country-house setting. Open 10am–5pm, closed Mon.

La Fonda €€ *Calle Nuestra Señora del Carmen 23, Pájara, tel: 928 161 471.* Opposite the church, La Fonda serves good island food – grilled rabbit and kid al salmorejo (with green peppers, in a herb and garlic marinade) and other dishes with *mojo* sauces. Closed Sun–Mon.

Caleta de Fuste

El Camarote €€ *Avenida del Castillo, tel: 928 163 100.* A pleasant place to sit and watch the world go by. The menu includes a range of local and international dishes served by helpful waiters. Open daily noon–10pm.

Maxorata €€ *Avenida del Castillo s/n, tel: 928 547 517*, www.barcelo.com. Good buffet restaurant serving local as well as international dishes located in the Barceló Fuerteventura Thalasso Spa hotel.

O'Fado €€ *Castillo Centre, tel: 928 163 369*. A Portuguese restaurant that's been here since 1996. Specialises in cod dishes, but has lots of other fish, meat and veggie options too.

SOUTHERN FUERTEVENTURA
La Pared

Bahía La Pared €€ *Playa de La Pared, tel: 928 549 030*. Great place, right on the beach with panoramic views from the terrace. The food's good, and there's a three-course set lunch menu (€).

Morro del Jable/Costa Calma

Mirador de Sotavento €€ *Cuesta de la Pared S/N, Costa Calma, tel: 692 06 65 82*. In a beautiful location, right by the sea, just outside the holiday resort of Costa Calma. The view is breathtaking and the traditional Spanish cuisine is very tasty. A good spot to enjoy the sunset. Closed Wed.

La Laja €€ *Avenida Tomás Grau (Avenida del Mar), Morro del Jable, tel: 928 166 080*. Great fish stews such as *sancocho canario*, grilled mussels with garlic, and other seafood, including some special *parrilladas* (huge plates of grilled seafood), served in a beach-side restaurant with a laid-back atmosphere. Closed Sat–Sun.

Saavedra Clavijo €€ *Avenida Tomás Grau (Avenida del Mar) Morro Jable, tel: 928 166 080*. This is a long established family-run place, with good fish, good atmosphere and very good prices. Open daily 10am–midnight.

A–Z TRAVEL TIPS

A SUMMARY OF PRACTICAL INFORMATION

A

ACCOMMODATION

Most accommodation on Lanzarote is in the three major resorts: Puerto del Carmen, Costa Teguise and Playa Blanca. Self-catering apartments are more common than hotel rooms, and are good value. Elsewhere, there is not a great deal of choice, although there are several acceptable hotels in Arrecife, and in the interior of both islands there is a growing number of *casas rurales* – rural properties that have been converted into small hotels or renovated and rented as self-catering accommodation. For information, contact www.rural-villas.com. You will not find budget accommodation in the resorts. Similarly in Fuerteventura, nearly all accommodation is in the main resorts (see page 135).

Hotels are rated from one-star to five-star Gran Lujo (GL). Prices within the categories may vary considerably. Breakfast is usually included in the rate. Package holidays are the most economical, offering accommodation in large, comfortable hotels and self-catering apartments, some known as aparthotels. It is wise to book in advance, especially around Christmas, Easter and July to August.

I would like a single/double room with/without bathroom and toilet/shower **Quisiera una habitación sencilla/ doble con/sin baño/ducha**
What's the rate per night? **¿Cuál es el precio por noche?**
Is breakfast included? **¿Está incluído el desayuno?**

AIRPORTS

Lanzarote's Arrecife's **Guacimeta** airport (ACE; www.aena.es) has two terminals. Terminal 1 services international flights. Thursday is 'change over' day in the resorts, which means the departures section can be very busy and best avoided if possible. The airport is about 6km (4 miles) west of Arrecife. There is a bus service to Arrecife about every half-hour (Route 22 Mon–Fri 7am–10.30pm, Route 23 Sat–Sun 7am–9pm; €1.40; tel: 928 811 522). No. 161 and 261 (weekdays only) run to Puerto del Carmen (€1.40) and Playa Blanca (€3.30).

A taxi from the airport to Arrecife costs about €18, to Puerto del Carmen around €22, to Costa Teguise €27 and to Playa Blanca €48, although may be more expensive if reserved in advance. Taxi drivers may charge extra fee for additional luggage (bikes, surfboards, etc). Arrecife airport information, tel: 913 211 000/902 404 704.

Taxi reservations, tel: 630 207 305, www.lanzarotetaxi.com.

Fuerteventura's modern and efficient airport **El Matorral** (FUE; www.aena.es) is about 7km (4 miles) south of Puerto del Rosario, about 9 km (6 miles) north of Caleta de Fuste. Bus No. 3 runs via Puerto del Rosario to Caleta de Fuste (€1.45; tel: 928 855 726) on weekdays from 6.30am–11.45pm and 7am–11.30pm at weekends. Buses no. 10 and 16 link the airport (via Puerto Rosario) with Morro Jable and Gran Tarajal respectively. Detailed schedules can be consulted at www.tiadhe.com/en/. A taxi from the airport to the capital costs about €14, to Caleta de Fuste about €16.

Fuerteventura airport information, tel: 913 211 000/902 404 704.

Taxi service, tel: 928 850 216/928 855 432.

B

BICYCLE HIRE

Road bikes, mountain bikes and scooters can be hired in most of the resorts (see page 87).

BUDGETING FOR YOUR TRIP

Accommodation: Rates for two sharing a double room in high season (July–August) can range from as low as €60 in a basic apartment or at a *pensión* or hostel (although there aren't many of these) to as much as €400 at a top-of-the-range five-star hotel. A pleasant three-star hotel will cost in the range of €100–€150. Rates drop considerably out of season, except at Christmas and Easter.

Attractions: The major attractions such as the Manrique sites and Cueva de los Verdes charge around €8–10; smaller museums around €5. More expensive are the family attractions such as the Jardín Tropical and the Aquapark (€22.50 per adult; €16 per child, aged 4–12 years).

Bike hire: between €10 and €15 a day, depending on the bike and the number of days for which it is hired.

Buses: eg. Arrecife to Puerto del Carmen €1.70 or Costa Teguise €1.40.

Car hire: Including comprehensive insurance and tax, rates are around €30–40 a day from the big international companies; you get a better deal if you book for a week (see page 119).

Getting there: Air fares vary enormously, with those from the UK to Lanzarote ranging between £100 in November to £350 in August (€111–€390), with spring and early-summer flights somewhere in between. From the US, flights cost from around $700. To Fuerteventura they range between £100 in November to around £250 (€111–280) in August – the lower summer price compared to Lanzarote due to the fact that there are *only* budget flights to Fuerteventura.

Meals and drinks: The cheap, three-course set meal called the *menú del día* is found less on these two islands than it is in most other parts of Spain. The average price of a three-course à la carte meal, including house wine, will be about €35 per person, but you can pay a lot less. At top restaurants you may pay nearly twice that.

Petrol: still cheap by UK standards – from €1 a litre.

Taxis: Prices are controlled, and reasonable. From Lanzarote airport to Puerto del Carmen the fare is around €22, while from Fuerteventura airport to Caleta de Fuste around €16.

C

CAMPING

There are two official campsites on Lanzarote (June–Sept only), but they do not offer much in the way of space or facilities:

Camping El Salao, Isla Graciosa, tel: 928 845 985/842 000. Tents only at this campsite with basic facilities (toilets/showers); no fires or barbecues. Camping is free, but as it is located in the national park, a permit and reservation is required. For more information, visit www.reservas-parquesnacionales.es.

Camping de Papagayo, Playa Blanca, tel: 640 294 179; €7 for a small tent pitch, €10 for trailers/caravans (June–Sept).

On Fuerteventura there are no official campsites, but rough camping is tolerated in some places; check with the local tourist office.

CAR HIRE (see also Driving)

You must be over 21, sometimes 24, to hire a car, and have held a licence for at least 12 months. You need your passport and a credit card. It is not easy to find a vehicle with automatic transmission. There are dozens of local companies in the resorts, and these tend to be cheaper, but check that cars are reliable and make sure you know what insurance you're getting: comprehensive with full damage waiver (*todo riesgo*) is more expensive but worthwhile. It may be cheaper to hire a car via the internet before you leave home. Cabrera Medina (tel: 928 822 900, www.cabreramedina.com) is the biggest and most respected of the local companies, with numerous outlets in the resorts, in Arrecife and

I'd like to rent a car for one day/week **Quisiera alquilar un coche por un día/una semana**

Please include full insurance. **Haga el favor de incluir el seguro a todo riesgo.**

at the airport. The big international companies all have offices at both islands' airports and in the resorts.

Avis: Lanzarote tel: 606 172 148, www.avis.es.

Europcar: Lanzarote airport tel: 928 846 260, www.europcar.es.

Hertz: Lanzarote airport tel: 928 846 190, www.hertz.es.

CLIMATE

The islands have an average annual temperature of 20°C (68°F), with mid-summer temperatures soaring to 30°C (86°F). There is very little rain – what there is mostly falls October–January.

CLOTHING

Light summer clothes, sandals and a swimsuit are all you need much of the time, but bring a sweater or jacket for cooler evenings and windy boat rides, and strong shoes if you want to do any walking. A jacket for men and a smart dress for women is appreciated, but not obligatory, in more expensive restaurants. Don't offend local sensibilities by wearing swimwear or skimpy clothing in city streets, museums or churches, although you can get away with almost anything in resorts.

CRIME AND SAFETY

Crime rates are not high, but there is some opportunistic bag-snatching and pickpocketing in busy tourist areas. Robberies from cars are the most prevalent, so never leave anything of value in your vehicle. Use the safe deposit box in your room for valuables, including your passport (carrying a photocopy is a good idea). Burglaries of holiday apartments do occur, too, so keep doors and windows locked when you are out. Report all thefts to the local police within 24 hours for your own insurance purposes.

I want to report a theft. **Quiero denunciar un robo.**

D

DISABLED TRAVELLERS

Arrecife and Fuerteventura airports and most modern hotels have wheelchair access and facilities for travellers with disabilities, but, generally speaking, facilities elsewhere are not good. For general information, consult the online *Able Magazine*, tel: (44) 141 285 4000, www.ablemagazine.co.uk. Tourism for All, tel: 0845 124 9971, www.tourismforall.org.uk also provides information.

DRIVING

Driving conditions: Main roads are generally well surfaced and signposted – although signage in the north of Lanzarote is a bit arbitrary. There are lots of roundabouts, but no traffic lights outside Arrecife. Drive on the right, pass on the left, yield right of way to vehicles coming from your left on roundabouts, but give way to vehicles coming from the right at junctions. Use your horn when approaching sharp bends. In rural areas you may come across a very slow tractor or a large pothole – even goats, in Fuerteventura.

Speed limits: 120kmh (75mph) on motorways, 100kmh (62mph) on dual carriageways, 90kmh (52mph) on primary roads, 50kmh (30mph) in built-up areas; 20kmh (12mph) in residential areas.

There are only a couple of stretches of motorway, around each of the capital cities and their airports, and they are toll-free.

Traffic and parking: In Arrecife traffic can be heavy, parking difficult and the one-way system confusing. Early afternoon is a good time to get in and out of town, and you are more likely to find a parking space. In Puerto del Rosario parking is rarely a problem. Elsewhere there are few traffic jams or parking problems.

It is an offence to park facing the traffic. Don't park on white or yellow lines. Blue lines indicate pay-and-display parking areas.

Petrol: Petrol is cheaper than in the UK and the rest of Europe. Un-leaded is *sin plomo*. A few of the larger petrol stations *(gasolineras)* are open 24 hours; most accept credit cards. In the interior of both islands there are fewer petrol stations, so don't run too low on fuel.

Regulations: Always carry your driving licence with you. Seat belts are compulsory. Children up to the age of 12 and less than 135cm tall must be provided with an appropriate child restraint. Don't use a mobile phone. Obviously, you should never drink and drive.

Traffic police: Armed Civil Guards (Guardia Civil) patrol the roads on motorcycles. In towns the municipal police handle traffic control. If you are fined for a traffic offence, you may have to pay on the spot or take your fine to the local town hall.

---

aparcamiento parking
desviación detour
obras roadworks
peatones pedestrians
peligro danger
salida de camiones truck exit
senso único one way
Useful expressions:
¿Se puede aparcar aquí? Can I park here?
Llénelo, por favor. Fill the tank please.
Ha habido un accidente. There has been an accident.

E

ELECTRICITY

220 volts is standard, with continental-style, two-pin sockets. Adaptors are available in UK shops and at airports. North American 110V appliances need a transformer.

EMBASSIES AND CONSULATES

Australia: (in Madrid), tel: 913 536 600.

Ireland: Calle León y Castillo 195, Las Palmas, tel: 928 297 728.
South Africa: Honorary Consulate, c/o Calle Albareda 54, Las Palmas, tel: 928 265 452.
UK: Calle Luis Morote 6–3, Las Palmas, tel: 928 262 508.
US: Calle Martínez Escobar 3, Las Palmas, tel: 928 271 259.

EMERGENCIES (see also Embassies, Health, Police)

General emergencies: **112**
National police: **091**
Local police: **092**
Guardia Civil: **062**
Traffic police: **928 315 575**
Ambulance: 112/**061**
Fire brigade: 112/**080**

Police! **¡Policía!**
Help! **¡Socorro!**
Fire! **¡Fuego!**
Stop! **¡Deténgase!**

G

GETTING THERE

By air: There are numerous budget airline flights direct from most UK airports to **Lanzarote** (easyJet, Ryanair, etc.). The flight time is about four hours. There are scheduled flights from London Heathrow (eg Iberia, www.iberia.com) that go via Madrid and/or Gran Canaria, which makes it a long journey.

There are not so many direct flight options to **Fuerteventura**, but Thomas Cook (www.flythomascook.com) and Jet2 (www.jet2.com) has a number of direct flights; flights operated by a number of other airlines can be found at Fuerteventura's airport website (www.aena.es).

At present there are no direct flights from the US, but several transatlantic carriers (American Airlines, Iberia, Air Europa), have flights via Madrid; the overall flight time is about 12 hours. Connections can also be made via London airports; check with a travel agency, or visit www.opodo.com.

Inter-island flights are operated by Binter Airlines (tel: 902 391 392, www.bintercanarias.com). The flight from Las Palmas de Gran Canaria to Arrecife takes about 45 minutes.

By ship: The Trasmediterránea ferry company runs a weekly service from Cádiz to Las Palmas de Gran Canaria and from there there are regular services to Puerto del Rosario and Arrecife (tel: 902 454 645 or check www.trasmediterranea.es). Naviera Armas (tel: 902 456 500 or 928 517 912 in Playa Blanca, www.navieraarmas.com) has regular services from Gran Canaria to Fuerteventura and to Lanzarote. Naviera Armas runs frequent ferries from Playa Blanca, Lanzarote, to Corralejo, Fuerteventura; crossings take about 35 minutes. The Fred Olsen Shipping Line, tel: 902 100 107 or 928 495 040, www.fredolsen.es, runs the *Bocayna Express* catamaran from Playa Blanca, Lanzarote, to Corralejo, Fuerteventura; journey time about 25 minutes.

H

HEALTH AND MEDICAL CARE

Non-EU visitors should always have private medical insurance, and although there are reciprocal arrangements between EU countries, it is advisable for UK citizens and other member nations to do the same, because the arrangements do not cover all eventualities. The European Health Insurance Card (EHIC) entitles UK citizens to reciprocal medical care. You can apply for one online (www.ehic.org. uk), by phone (tel: 0300 330 1350) or by picking up a form at a main post office. Only treatment provided under a state scheme is covered, so make sure the practitioner is working within the Spanish Health Service. Leave a photocopy of the card with the hospital or doctor. Dental treatment is not available under this system. Hotel receptionists or private clinics will be able to recommend dentists.

Hospitals: The main hospital in Arrecife is Hospital Insular, Juan de Quesada s/n (Puerto de Naos), tel: 928 810 000.

In Puerto del Rosario: Hospital General, Carretera General del Aeropuerto Km 1, tel: 928 862 124/59.

Red Cross (Cruz Roja): tel: 902 222 292, www.cruzroja.es.

Private clinics: In the resorts on both islands there are private clinics where you will have to pay for treatment on the spot and reclaim it on your medical insurance. Most have English-speaking staff.

Lanzarote:

Hospiten Lanzarote (www.hospiten.com) is a private hospital on Lomo Gordo, Puerto del Carmen, tel: 928 596 100.

Branches of Dr. Mager Clinics (www.lanzamedic.com) offer 24-hour service. The 24-hour emergency number is tel: 649 973 366. Clinics are located at:

Costa Teguise: Avenida Islas Canarias, tel: 928 826 072.

Puerto del Carmen: Avenida de las Playas 37, Puerto del Carmen, tel: 928 512 611.

Where's the nearest (all-night) chemist? **¿Dónde está la farmacia (de guardia) más cercana?**
I need a doctor/dentist **Necesito un médico/dentista**
sunburn **quemadura del sol**
sunstroke **una insolación**
a fever **fiebre**
an upset stomach **molestias de estómago**

Playa Blanca: Avenida Llegada 1, tel: 928 517 938.

Fuerteventura:

Caleta de Fuste: Clínica Médica Dr. Bludau, Calle La Galera 1, Urb. Pueblo de los Pescadores, tel: 928 163 732.

Corralejo: Centro Médico Brisamar, Calle Nuestra Señora del Carmen, tel: 928 536 402.

Costa Calma: Centro Medico Jandia, Hotel Taro Beach, Calle LTU 1, tel: 928 541 543.

Puerto Rosario: Calle Virgen de la Peña, Esq. Calle Murillo 59, Puerto del Rosario, tel: 928 530 120.

Farmacias: Most problems visitors experience are due to too much sun, too much alcohol, or food they are unused to. These problems can often be dealt with by *farmacias* (chemists), identified by a green cross. Spanish pharmacists are highly trained and can often dispense medicines over the counter that would need a prescription in the UK. They are open during normal shopping hours, and one in each town, the *farmacia de guardia*, remains open all night. Its location is posted in the window of other *farmacias* and in local papers.

L

LANGUAGE

The Spanish spoken in the Canary Islands is slightly different from that of the mainland. A number of Latin American words and expressions are used. The most common are *guagua* (pronounced *wah-wah*), meaning bus, and *papa* (potato). Also, islanders don't lisp when they pronounce the letters *c* or *z*. In tourist areas basic English, German and some French is spoken, or at least understood. The *Berlitz Spanish Phrasebook & Dictionary* covers most of the situations you may encounter.

LGBTQ TRAVELLERS

The people of the Canary Islands generally have a tolerant attitude and there are a number of gay bars in the resorts. For information, visit www.lanzarotegayguide.com, www.gaywelcome.com or www. gcgay.com.

M

MAPS

Most tourist offices, and some of the larger hotels, will give you free maps, which should be sufficient, and hire car agencies usually provide a basic road map. If you want something more detailed, you can find road maps in most gift/souvenir shops and supermarkets.

> Do you have a map of the city/island? **¿Tiene un plano de la ciudad/isla?**

MEDIA

Radio and television *(radio; televisión)*: Many hotels have satellite TV with several stations in various languages, including CNN. TV Canarias is a local station which includes some English-language news and tourist information in its programming. English-language radio stations include Radio 40 Principales FM 100.4 MHz; Power FM 98.2 MHz; UK Away FM 99.9 MHz and 99.4 MHz.

Newspapers and magazines *(periódicos; revistas)*: Major British and German tabloids are on sale in the resorts on the day of publication, but English broadsheet newspapers are a bit more scarce. British and German magazines are widely available.

The online English-language Island Connections (www.islandcon nections.eu) has island news and tourist information but concentrates mainly on Gran Canaria and Tenerife.

For anyone who speaks Spanish, the island newspapers are *Canari-*

> Where's the nearest bank/currency exchange office?
> **¿Dónde está el banco más cercano/la casa de cambio más cercana?**
> I want to change some dollars/pounds **Quiero cambiar dólares/libras esterlinas**
> Do you accept traveller's cheques? **¿Acepta usted cheques de viajero?**
> Can I pay with this credit card? **¿Puedo pagar con esta tarjeta de crédito?**

as7 and *La Provincia*. Both of these contain listings of events so they can be useful.

MONEY

Currency: The monetary unit in the Canary Islands, as throughout Spain, is the euro, abbreviated €. Banknotes are available in denominations of €500, 200, 100, 50, 20, 10 and 5. The euro is subdivided into 100 cents, and there are coins available for €1 and €2 and for 50, 20, 10, 5, 2 and 1 cent.

Currency exchange: Banks are the preferred place to exchange currency, but *casas de cambio* also change money, as do some travel agencies, and these stay open outside banking hours. Larger hotels may change guests' money, but the rate is less advantageous. Banks and exchange offices pay less for cash than for traveller's cheques. Always take your passport when changing money.

Credit cards: Major international cards are widely recognised, although smaller businesses tend to prefer cash. Visa/Eurocard/MasterCard are most generally accepted. Credit and debit cards, with a PIN number, are also useful for obtaining euros from ubiquitous ATMs. They offer the most convenient way of obtaining cash, and will usually give you the best exchange rate.

O

OPENING TIMES

Banks usually open Monday to Friday 8am–2pm; large ones may also open on Saturday. Shops and offices are usually open Monday to Saturday, 10am–1 or 1.30pm, 5–8.30pm (although some close on Saturday afternoon). Large supermarkets may stay open all day and until 10pm, as do many shops in the tourist resorts, and some also open on Sunday. Post offices open Monday to Saturday 8.30am–2pm.

P

POLICE (see also Emergencies)

There are three police forces in the Canary Islands, as in the rest of Spain. The green-uniformed Guardia Civil (Civil Guard) is the main force. Each town also has its own Policía Municipal (municipal police), whose uniform can vary but is mostly blue and grey. The third force, the Cuerpo Nacional de Policía, is a national anti-crime unit that sports a light brown uniform. All police officers are armed. Spanish police are strict but courteous to foreign visitors.

National police: **091** or **928 597 107**

Guardia Civil: **062**

Where's the nearest police station? **¿Dónde está la comisaría más cercana?**

POST OFFICES

Post offices usually open Monday to Friday 8.30am–2.30pm and 9am–1pm on Sat; some stay open longer (for instance office in Arrecife on Avenida La Marina 8; 8.30am–8.30pm), but it is better not to count on it. They are for mail, not telephone calls. The main post office in Arrecife is at Avenida de Marina 8. In Costa Teguise, it's in the Centro Comercial Maretas on Avenida Islas Canarias, almost opposite the police station. In Puerto del Carmen, it's on Avenida Juan Carlos I s/n; in Playa Blanca, Avenida El Correlillo s/n. On Fuerteventura, Puerto del Rosario's post office is at Calle Canalejas 2; in Morro Jable, the post office can be found on Calle Buenavista s/n.

Stamps *(sellos)* are also sold at any tobacconist *(estanco)* and by most shops selling postcards, including supermarkets in the resorts. Mailboxes are painted yellow. If one of the slots is marked *extranjero*, it is for letters abroad.

> Where is the (nearest) post office? **¿Dónde está la oficina de correos (más cercana)?**
> A stamp for this letter/postcard, please **Por favor, un sello para esta carta/tarjeta**

PUBLIC HOLIDAYS

1 January *Año Nuevo* New Year's Day
6 January *Día de los Reyes* Epiphany
1 May *Día del Trabajo* Labour Day
30 May *Día de las Islas Canarias* Canary Islands' Day
16 July *Nuestra Señora del Carmen* Our Lady of Carmen
25 July *Santiago Apóstol* St James' Day
15 August *Asunción* Assumption Day
12 October *Día de la Hispanidad* National Day
1 November *Todos los Santos* All Saints' Day
6 December *Día de la Constitución* Constitution Day
8 December *Inmaculada Concepción* Immaculate Conception
25 December *Navidad* Christmas Day

Movable dates:

Carnaval Officially pre-Lent but different towns celebrate at different times so dates do not clash.

Jueves Santo Maundy Thursday.

Viernes Santo Good Friday.

Corpus Christi Corpus Christi (mid-June).

T

TAXES

A sales tax, the Impuesto Generalisado Indirecto Canario (IGIC) is levied on all bills at a rate of 7 percent. The tax may be included in the price you are quoted for hotel rooms, but usually it is not.

TELEPHONES

Phone booths (*kioskos*) accept coins and cards (*tarjetas telefónicas*), available from tobacconists, hotels and machines that you will see in all the shopping centres. Instructions in English and area/country codes are displayed clearly in phone booths. International calls are expensive, so have a plentiful supply of coins or use a card. *Cabinas* or *locutorios* – cabins where you make a call and then pay at a desk afterwards – are a convenient way of making long-distance calls. Calling from your hotel room is expensive. Calls from your mobile (cell) phones are generally the least expensive, unless you are using a phone from outside the EU.

For international calls, wait for the dial tone, then dial 00, wait for a second tone and dial the country code, area code (minus any initial zero) and the number. **International Operator**: 025.

Country codes: Australia 61, Ireland 353, New Zealand 64, UK 44, US and Canada 1.

Telephone codes for the Canary Islands (which must always be dialled, even for local calls): Gran Canaria, Lanzarote and Fuerteventura 928; Tenerife, El Hierro, La Gomera and La Palma 922.

TIME ZONES

The time in the Canaries is the same as in the UK, Greenwich Mean Time, but one hour behind the rest of Europe, including Spain, and five hours ahead of New York. Like the rest of Europe, the islands adopt summer time (putting the clocks forward by an hour) from the end of March through to the end of September.

TIPPING

A service charge is sometimes included in restaurant bills (look for the words *servicio incluído*). If it is not included, then add around 10 percent, which is also the usual tip for taxi drivers and hairdressers. In bars, customers usually leave a few coins, rounding up the bill. A hotel porter will appreciate €1 for carrying heavy bags to your room; tip hotel maids according to your length of stay.

TOILETS

Public conveniences are rare. The proprietors of some bars and restaurants do not mind if you drop in to use their facilities, but it is polite to buy something, even if it is only a bottle of water. Others keep the key behind the bar to make sure their toilets are not used by the general public or, if they are, that users pay a small sum.

> Where are the lavatories? **¿Dónde están los servicios?**

TOURIST INFORMATION OFFICES

Information on the Canary Islands can be found at www.spain.info or Spanish National Tourist Offices, including:

Canada: 2 Bloor Street West, Suite 3402, Toronto, Ontario M4W 3E2, Canada, tel: 1416/9613131-1416/9614079.

UK: 64 North Row, 6th floor, London W1K 7DE, tel: 020-7317 2011, www. spain.info/en_GB/.

US: Water Tower Place, Suite 915 East, 845 North Michigan Avenue, Chicago, IL 60611, tel: 312-642 1992; 8383 Wilshire Boulevard, Suite 960, Beverly Hills, CA 90211, tel: 213-658 7188; 60 East 42nd Street, Suite 5300, New York, NY 10103, tel: 212-265 8822.

Tourist offices on the islands: (open approx. 9.30am–1.30pm)

Lanzarote:

Airport: tel: 928 820 704.

Arrecife: Parque José Ramírez Cerdá, tel: 928 813 174.

Costa Teguise: Avenida de las Islas Canarias, tel: 928 592 542.

Playa Blanca: El Varadero 3, tel: 928 519 238.

Puerto del Carmen: Avenida de las Playas s/n (next to the Fundación Manrique shop), tel: 928 513 351.

Fuerteventura:

Airport: tel: 928 860 604.

Caleta de Fuste: Avenida Juan Ramón Soto Morales 10, Centro Comercial Castillo, tel: 928 163 286.

Corralejo: Avenida Marítima 2, tel: 928 866 235.

Morro Jable: Centro Comercial Cosmo, Avenida El Saladar, Local 88, tel: 928 540 776.

Puerto del Rosario: Avenida Reyes de España s/n, tel: 928 850 110.

TRANSPORT

There is no train service on either island. The **bus services** are cheap and reliable but really only useful for getting from the two islands' capital cities to the main resorts. Buses between towns are infrequent, although there are some useful services in the south of Fuerteventura.

Lanzarote: tel: 928 811 522, http://intercitybuslanzarote.es.

Fuerteventura: tel: 928 855 726, www.tiadhe.com.

(For inter-island ferries and flights, see page 124.)

Taxis: The letters SP (*servicio público*) on the front and rear bumpers of a car indicate that it is a taxi. It may also have a green light in the front windscreen or a green sign indicating *'libre'* when it is free. Fares are metered, but for longer, out-of-town journeys you may feel happier if you agree an approximate fare in advance. Taxis are good value (initial price €3.15, than € 0.55 per kilometre).

Lanzarote: Lanzarote Taxi, tel: 630 207 305, www.lanzarotetaxi.com.

Fuerteventura: Fuertventura Taxi, tel: 928 850 216, www.taxis fuerteventura.es.

V

VISAS AND ENTRY REQUIREMENTS

Citizens of EU countries, the US, Canada, Ireland, Australia and New Zealand need only a valid passport. No inoculations are required. The islands are part of the EU but there is a restriction on duty-free goods that can be brought back to the UK. The allowance is 200 cigarettes or 50 cigars or 250g tobacco; 1 litre spirits over 22 percent or 2 litres under 22 percent, and 2 litres of wine.

W

WATER

The islands suffer from water shortage, so try not to waste it. Don't drink tap water. Inexpensive bottled water is available everywhere. *Con gas* is sparkling, *sin gas* is still.

WEBSITES AND INTERNET ACCESS

www.ecoturismocanarias.com natural parks and rural tourism.

www.rural-villas.com for attractive rural villas and apartments.

http://visitfuerteventura.es helpful site for general information.

www.lanzaroteguidebook.com lots of general information.

www.turismolanzarote.com official Lanzarote tourism site.

Internet: There are internet cafés in all the resorts, usually in the big commercial centres, although they tend to come and go. Most hotels now have internet access in their public areas and some now offer free Wi-Fi as well.

RECOMMENDED HOTELS

Most accommodation on both islands is concentrated in the resorts. Elsewhere, there is not a great deal of choice, although there are some delightful casas rurales (rural hotels) in the island interiors (check www.rural-villas.com), and several very acceptable ones in Arrecife. You will find very little budget accommodation in the resorts. Self-catering apartments are ubiquitous and good value. Most are in holiday complexes, some called aparthotels, and usually offer hotel facilities such as a pool, restaurant, etc. You can also rent an apartment on a bed-and-breakfast or half-board basis.

Prices are for two sharing a double room, or a one-bedroomed apartment, in high season (July–August and Christmas/New Year; some rural casas charge high-season rates in autumn). Breakfast is usually included in the rates. Tax (IGIC) is extra if you book independently, but included if you book a package. Prices are approximate only, and if you take a package deal you will usually pay considerably less.

€€€€	over €200
€€€	€120–200
€€	€70–120
€	below €70

LANZAROTE: ARRECIFE

Arrecife Gran Hotel & Spa €€€ *Parque Islas Canarias, tel: 928 800 000*, www.aghotelspa.com. This 17-storey hotel, completely renovated, is smart and glossy, with a conference room, shops, a hairdressing salon, swimming pool, sauna and gym, underground parking and stunning views from the restaurant/bar on the top floor and from many of the well-furnished rooms and suites.

Lancelot €€ *Calle Mancomunidad 9, tel: 928 805 099*, www.hotellancelot. com. A pleasant modern hotel right by the Reducto beach, with babysitting services, a pool and a restaurant with sea views. A convenient base for a short stay. Has some good half-board offers.

NORTHERN LANZAROTE
Haría

Casitas Tabayesco €€ *Calle Chafariz 26, Haría, tel: 645 040 829*, www.casitas tabayesco.com. In the greenest part of Lanzarote, this agreeable little guest-house is located in a beautiful village of Tabayesco. One villa and several houses to rent, each with kitchen, living room and a rooftop terrace, perfect for sunbathing or breakfast. The hosts, Rich and Carolina, are very helpful.

Arte de Obra €–€€ *Calle San Juan 12, Yé (Haría), tel: 928 835 405*; www.arte deobra.com. Three colourful rooms and three apartments, with a communal kitchen and garden, in an art center in Haría. Some rooms have shared bathrooms and two of the apartments have a sea view. The German host, Bettina, knows how to create a good ambience and is happy to share her knowledge about the island and César Manrique whom she knew personally.

Isla Graciosa

Apartamentos El Sombrerito € *Calle Sirena 71, Caleta del Sebo, mobile: 696 942 874*, www.elsombrerito.com. Seven simple apartments a stone's throw from the harbour. Perfect peace. Minimum stay of 7 nights in high season.

Evita Beach Apartamentos €–€€ *Avenida Virgen del Mar 59, Caleta del Sebo, tel: 625 339 586*, www.evitabeach.club. Right by the harbour, there are eight apartments with one, two or three rooms decorated in different styles. The accommodation is clean and roomy with great sea views.

CENTRAL LANZAROTE
Costa Teguise

Apartamentos Celeste € *Avenida de las Islas Canarias 21–23–25, tel: 928 591 720*, www.apartmentsceleste.com. Simple, pleasant apartments in an attractive building that is part of the pretty Pueblo Marinero, the nicest area in the resort. Very close to the beach.

Barceló La Galea €€€ *Paseo Marítimo s/n, tel: 928 590 551, from UK: 0 8000 211 256*, www.barcelo.com. Comfortable, well-equipped studios and apartments arranged around a pool in an attractive low-rise complex, built in traditional, Manrique-approved style by the beach at the west end of Playa de las Cucharas. All-inclusive packages available.

Gran Meliá Salinas €€€€ *Avenida de las Islas Canarias s/n, tel: 928 590 040, from the UK: 0808 234 1953*, www.melia.com. Right on the beach, this hotel has luxurious rooms, faultless service, and a wonderful lobby and atrium created by Manrique, with pools, tropical foliage and statuary. Hibiscus flowers are scattered everywhere, even in the marble-walled toilets.

Lanzarote Gardens €€€ *Avenida de las Islas Canarias 13, tel: 928 590 100*, www.hotelh10lanzarotegardens.com. One- and two-bedroomed fully serviced apartments in attractive gardens grouped around two pools, just back from Playa de las Cucharas. All rooms have balconies. Restaurant, poolside bar. Children's entertainment every evening, and a small playground and children's pool area. Efficient, multilingual staff. Also offers full-board packages.

Mozaga/San Bartolomé

Caserio de Mozaga €€ *Mozaga, tel: 928 520 060*, www.caseriodemozaga. com. An 18th-century farmhouse with a flower-filled courtyard and eight double rooms with tiled floors, wood-beamed ceilings and traditional furniture. Tradition is complemented with modernity: air-conditioning and internet access in the rooms. Great breakfasts and an excellent restaurant, open to the public (see page 125).

Finca de la Florida €€ *El Islote 90, San Bartolomé, tel: 928 521 124*, www. hotelfincalaflorida.com. In the wine-producing area of La Geria, about 2km (1.2 miles) from the Monumento del Campesino, this attractive blue-and-white hotel offers comfortably furnished double rooms and suites. Gym, sauna, pool, jacuzzi, and tennis and mountain bikes are available, but its biggest asset is the amazing view.

Puerto del Carmen

Nautilus Lanzarote € *Calle Gramillo 5, tel: 928 512 390*, www.nautilus-lanzarote.com. All of these nicely furnished, one or two bedroom apartments have a private terrace. The complex has a mini golf court, billiards, table tennis, children's playground, library, a small supermarket and two pools. The grounds are immaculate and the staff are very friendly. It's just 10 minutes' drive from the airport.

La Geria €€–€€€ *Calle Jupiter 5, Playa de los Pocillos, tel: 928 510 441*, www.hipotels.com. Pleasant four-storey hotel at the quieter end of the resort. Rooms have sea views to the side, or garden/pool views. There is a landscaped pool area.

Los Cocoteros €€ *Avenida de las Playas 23, tel: 928 510 361*, www.loscocoteroslanzarote.com. Pleasant white block with Gaudí-esque chimneys. Well-equipped serviced apartments with patios. Most have sea views.

Los Fariones €€€ *Calle Roque del Este 1, tel: 928 59 57 02*, www.farioneshotels.com. This huge, comfortable 1960s hotel is right beside the beach at the harbour end of the resort, set in lush gardens. Pool and tennis court. Under renovation at the time of writing.

Los Jameos Playa €€€–€€€€ *Calle Marte 2, Playa de los Pocillos s/n, tel: 928 511 717*, www.los-jameos-playa.es. A large, light hotel with Canarian-style balconies in the spacious reception area. Rooms built around a series of airy white-painted courtyards.

Vik Hotel San Antonio €€–€€€ *Avenida de las Playas 84, tel: 902 160 630*, www.vikhotels.com. Located at the point between Playa Grande and Playa de los Pocillos, where the road becomes quieter and more residential. It looks rather clinical from outside, but it is extremely comfortable and well run. Most of the rooms have sea views.

SOUTHERN LANZAROTE
Playa Blanca

Casa del Embajador €€€€ *Calle La Tegala 56, tel: 928 519 191*, www.hotelcasadelembajador.com. Unusual in Playa Blanca, this is a family-run hotel in an old house that once belonged to a diplomat (hence the name). Right by the beach, it has just 12 rooms and one suite, all well-furnished and decorated. There's lots of atmosphere and wonderful views across to Fuerteventura.

Hotel Volcán Lanzarote €€€–€€€€ *Urbanización Castillo de Águila s/n, tel: 928 519 185*, www.hotelvolcanlanzarote.com. Spacious and luxurious, this hotel, which overlooks the Marina Rubicón yacht harbour, has 251 rooms, all with terrraces or balconies, located in 20 separate buildings. There are three conference rooms, five restaurants, several bars, four pools, a gym and spa.

Lanzarote Princess €€€ *Calle Maciot s/n, tel: 928 517 108*, www.hotelh10lanzaroteprincess.com. Part of the reliable H10 chain, this hotel is set back a couple of hundred metres from Playa Dorada beach. The air-conditioned rooms all have terraces or balconies. There are two restaurants, a café and two bars, plus two pools, a tennis court, volleyball, children's facilities and entertainment.

Princess Yaiza €€€€ *Avenida Papagayo 22, tel: 928 519 300*, www.princesayaiza.com. Right on the beach, this smart hotel has a strong Hispano-Arabic theme to the architecture. Five restaurants offer Japanese, Italian and Mexican food, among other styles. There's a spa, gym, pools, squash, tennis, and Kikoland, a children's playground. Minimum four nights' stay.

Timanfaya Palace €€€ *Gran Canaria 1, Montaña Roja, tel: 928 517 676*, www.hotelh10timanfayapalace.com. This hotel on Playa Flamingo has Arabic-style architecture, comfortable rooms, billiards/snooker, gym and all-weather tennis court, plus babysitting services, children's play area; free Wi-fi in public areas.

Uga/Yaiza

Casa El Morro €€–€€€ *El Morro 1, Uga, tel: 928 830 392*, http://casael morro.com. Perched on a hillside, this attractive complex offers modern comfort in a traditional 18th-century building. There are several individually decorated *casitas* surrounded by palms and bougainvillea, ranged round a courtyard; small pool, views over volcanic hills and lots of peace and tranquillity.

Casona de Yaiza €€€ *Calle El Rincón s/n, Yaiza, tel: 928 836 262*, www.casonadeyaiza.com. Attractively furnished rooms, heated pool and jacuzzi, good restaurant in the old wine cellar, gardens full of palms and cacti. The underground cisterns – *aljibes* – have become a small art gallery.

Casa de Hilario €€€€ *Calle General Garcia Escamez, 19, Yaiza, tel: 928 836 262*. Cosy rooms equipped with large showers and well-designed furniture. The pool in a small courtyard is surrounded by cactuses. A good breakfast is served on the sunny terrace. Amazing views of the coast.

Finca Malvasia €€–€€€ *Masdache, La Geria, tel: 692 155 981/665 468 538*, www.fincamalvasia.com. Four individually designed, whitewashed apartments with terraces are set in tastefully landscaped gardens around a pool in the heart of a working vineyard, with a backdrop of volcanic Timanfaya.

FUERTEVENTURA: PUERTO DEL ROSARIO

Hotel Fuerteventura Playa Blanca €€ *Playa Blanca, tel: 928 851 150*. This former parador stands alone, right on the beach between the capital and the airport. In a distinctive building, it offers excellent service and ocean views.

Puerto Rosario JM Palace €€ *Avenida Marítima 9, tel: 928 859 464*, www.jmhoteles.com. Opposite the port, this modern hotel has comfortable, air-conditioned rooms and friendly, obliging staff.

NORTHERN FUERTEVENTURA
Corralejo

Corralejo Beach €–€€ *Calle Victor Grau Bassas, tel: 928 535 651*, www.corralejobeach.com. Pleasant, functional one- and two-room apartments and two suites, close to the beach.

Riu Palace Tres Islas €€–€€€ *Avenida Grandes Playas, tel: 928 535 700/ 801 080 996*, www.riu.com. Huge hotel, on the edge of the dunes, 5km (3 miles) from the town centre, with gym, tennis and all the facilities and comforts you would expect, indoors and out. Piano bar and children's daytime entertainment.

El Cotillo/Villaverde

Casa Vieja Hotel Boutique & Villas Oasis €€ *General De La Oliva s/n, tel: 928 535 159*, www.oasiscasavieja.com. Small hotel, with just ten rooms located around two patios and surrounded by a nice garden. There are also villas, which sleep four to six people, available for rent. Shared pool.

Hotel Rural Mahoh €–€€ *Sitio Juan Bello s/n, Villaverde, La Oliva, tel: 928 868 050*, www.mahoh.com. Early 19th-century house built of volcanic stone, with gardens, pool and multi-purpose sports pitch. Bedrooms furnished in traditional style. Environmentally-aware owners. Only about 10 minutes' drive from beaches of El Cotillo and Corralejo.

CENTRAL FUERTEVENTURA
Caleta de Fuste

Barceló Club El Castillo €€€ *Avenida El Castillo, tel: 928 163 100*, www.barcelo.com. This well-landscaped beach-side complex has pretty bungalows set in gardens; pools for adults and children, a children's playground and several restaurants. Terms can be self-catering, B&B, half-board or all-inclusive.

Casa Isaítas €€ *Calle Guize 7, Pájara, tel: 928 161 402*, www.casaisaitas. com. A delightful place, white-walled with Canarian balconies and a pretty courtyard. There is a good restaurant, and delicious breakfasts.

Elba Castillo San Jorge & Antigua Suite Hotel €€ *Calle Franch y Roca s/n, tel: 902 172 182*, www.hoteleselba.com. About 500m/yds from the beach and the same distance from the town centre, this large apartho-tel offers comfortable accommodation, in a complex with pools, sauna, restaurants and bars.

SOUTHERN FUERTEVENTURA
Jandía Playa

Barceló Jandía Playa €€€ *Calle La Mancha s/n, Barranco de Vinamar, tel: 928 546 000*, www.barcelo.com. Large hotel complex a few minutes from Morro del Jable. All modern comforts in an attractive setting, plus four pools, a gym, solarium, a wellness centre, children's club, bars and three restaurants.

Hotel Meliá Gorriones €€€ *Playa la Barca, tel: 928 547 025, from UK: 0808-234 195*, www.solmelia.com. In a quiet spot at the start of the Jandía Peninsula, this large hotel offers everything you need for a relaxed and comfortable beach holiday, and it is the base for the ac-claimed René Egli Windsurf School (www.rene-egli.com). Minimum two-night stay.

Iberostar Playa Gaviotas Hotel €€€–€€€€ *Pasaje Playa 2, Jandía, tel: 928 166 197/912 764 747*, www.iberostar.com. Pleasant all-inclusive hotel right on the beach; air-conditioned rooms with terraces, restaurant, cocktail bar, two pools and children's pool. There are 16 family rooms and 6 rooms adapted for people with disabilities.

DICTIONARY

adj adjective   **adv** adverb   **BE** British English   **n** noun   **prep** preposition   **v** verb

A

abbey la abadía
accept v aceptar
access el acceso
accident el accidente
accommodation el alojamiento
account la cuenta
acupuncture la acupuntura
adapter el adaptador
address la dirección
admission la entrada
after después;
   ~noon la tarde;
   ~shave el bálsamo para después del afeitado
age la edad
agency la agencia
AIDS el sida
air el aire; **~ conditioning** el aire acondicionado;
   ~ pump el aire;
   ~line la compañía aérea; **~mail** el correo aéreo; **~plane** el avión; **~port** el aeropuerto
aisle el pasillo; **~ seat** el asiento de pasillo
allergic alérgico; **~ reaction** la reacción alérgica

allow v permitir
alone solo
alter v (clothing) hacer un arreglo
alternate route el otro camino
aluminum foil el papel de aluminio
amazing increíble
ambulance la ambulancia
American estadounidense
amusement park el parque de atracciones
anemic anémico
anesthesia la anestesia
animal el animal
ankle el tobillo
antibiotic el antibiótico
antiques store la tienda de -antigüedades
antiseptic cream la crema antiséptica
anything algo
apartment el apartamento
appendix (body part) el apéndice
appetizer el aperitivo
appointment la cita
arcade el salón de juegos recreativos

area code el prefijo
arm el brazo
aromatherapy la aromaterapia
around (the corner) doblando (la esquina)
arrivals (airport) las llegadas
arrive v llegar
artery la arteria
arthritis la artritis
arts las letras
Asian asiático
aspirin la aspirina
asthmatic asmático
ATM el cajero automático
attack el asalto
attend v asistir
attraction (place) el sitio de interés
attractive guapo
Australia Australia
Australian australiano
automatic automático;
   ~ car coche automático
available disponible

B

baby el bebé; **~ bottle** el biberón;
   ~ wipe la toallita;
   ~sitter el/la canguro
back la espalda;

~ache el dolor de espalda; **~pack** la mochila
bag la maleta
baggage el equipaje; **~ claim** la recogida de equipajes; **~ ticket** el talón de equipaje
bakery la panadería
ballet el ballet
bandage la tirita
bank el banco
bar el bar
barbecue la barbacoa
barber la peluquería de caballeros
baseball el béisbol
basket (grocery store) la cesta
basketball el baloncesto
bathroom el baño
battery (car) la batería
battery la pila
battleground el campo de batalla
be v ser, estar
beach la playa
beautiful precioso
bed la cama; **~ and breakfast** la pensión
begin v empezar
before antes de

beginner principiante
behind detrás de
beige beis
belt el cinturón
berth la litera
best el/la mejor
better mejor
bicycle la bicicleta
big grande
bigger más grande
bike route el sendero para bicicletas
bikini el biquini; ~ **wax** la depilación de las ingles
bill v **(charge)** cobrar; ~ n **(money)** el billete; ~ n **(of sale)** el recibo
bird el pájaro
birthday el cumpleaños
black negro
bladder la vejiga
bland soso
blanket la manta
bleed v sangrar
blood la sangre; ~ **pressure** la tensión arterial
blouse la blusa
blue azul
board v embarcar
boarding pass la tarjeta de embarque
boat el barco
bone el hueso
book el libro; ~**store** la librería
boots las botas
boring aburrido
botanical garden el jardín botánico
bother v molestar

bottle la botella; ~ **opener** el abrebotellas
bowl el cuenco
box la caja
boxing match la pelea de boxeo
boy el niño; ~**friend** el novio
bra el sujetador
bracelet la pulsera
brakes (car) los frenos
break v romper
break-in (burglary) el allanamiento de morada
breakdown la avería
breakfast el desayuno
breast el seno; ~**feed** dar el pecho
breathe v respirar
bridge el puente
briefs (clothing) los calzoncillos
bring v traer
British británico
broken roto
brooch el broche
broom la escoba
brother el hermano
brown marrón
bug el insecto
building el edificio
burn v **(CD)** grabar
bus el autobús; ~ **station** la estación de autobuses; ~ **stop** la parada de autobús; ~ **ticket** el billete de autobús; ~ **tour** el recorrido en autobús
business los negocios; ~ **card** la tarjeta de negocios; ~ **cent-**

er el centro de negocios; ~ **class** la clase preferente; ~ **hours** el horario de atención al público
butcher el carnicero
buttocks las nalgas
buy v comprar
bye adiós

C

cabaret el cabaré
cabin (house) la cabaña; ~ **(ship)** el camarote
cable car el teleférico
cafe la cafetería
call v llamar; ~ n la llamada
calories las calorías
camera la cámara; **digital** ~ la cámara digital; ~ **case** la funda para la cámara; ~ **store** la tienda de fotografía
camp v acampar; ~ **stove** el hornillo; ~**site** el cámping
can opener el abrelatas
Canada Canadá
Canadian canadiense
cancel v cancelar
candy el caramelo
canned goods las conservas
canyon el cañón
car el coche; ~ **hire [BE]** el alquiler de coches; ~ **park [BE]** el aparcamiento; ~ **rental** el alquiler de coches; ~ **seat** el

asiento de niño
carafe la garrafa
card la tarjeta; **ATM** ~ la tarjeta de cajero automático; **credit** ~ la tarjeta de crédito; **debit** ~ la tarjeta de débito; **phone** ~ la tarjeta telefónica
carry-on (piece of hand luggage) el equipaje de mano
cart (grocery store) el carrito; ~ **(luggage)** el carrito para el equipaje
carton el cartón; ~ **of cigarettes** el cartón de tabaco
case (amount) la caja
cash v cobrar; ~ n el efectivo; ~ **advance** sacar dinero de la tarjeta
cashier el cajero
casino el casino
castle el castillo
cathedral la catedral
cave la cueva
CD el CD
cell phone el teléfono móvil
Celsius el grado centígrado
centimeter el centímetro
certificate el certificado
chair la silla; ~ **lift** el telesilla
change v **(buses)** cambiar; ~ n **(money)** el cambio
charcoal el carbón

charge v (credit card) cobrar; ~ n (cost) el precio

cheap barato

cheaper más barato

check v (on something) revisar; ~ v (luggage) facturar; ~ n (payment) el cheque; **~-in** (airport) la facturación; **~-in** (hotel) el registro; **~ing account** la cuenta corriente; **~-out** (hotel) la salida

Cheers! ¡Salud!

chemical toilet el váter químico

chemist [BE] la farmacia

cheque [BE] el cheque

chest (body part) el pecho; **~ pain** el dolor de pecho

chewing gum el chicle

child el niño; **~ seat** la silla para niños

children's menu el menú para niños

children's portion la ración para niños

Chinese chino

chopsticks los palillos chinos

church la iglesia

cigar el puro

cigarette el cigarrillo

class la clase; **business ~** la clase preferente; **economy ~** la clase económica; **first ~** la primera clase

classical music la música clásica

clean v limpiar; ~ adj limpio; **~ing product** el producto de limpieza; **~ing supplies** los productos de limpieza

clear v (on an ATM) borrar

cliff el acantilado

cling film [BE] el film transparente

close v (a shop) cerrar

closed cerrado

clothing la ropa; **~ store** la tienda de ropa

club la discoteca

coat el abrigo

coffee shop la cafetería

coin la moneda

colander el escurridor

cold n (sickness) el catarro; ~ adj (temperature) frío

colleague el compañero de trabajo

cologne la colonia

color el color

comb el peine

come v venir

complaint la queja

computer el ordenador

concert el concierto; **~ hall** la sala de conciertos

condition (medical) el estado de salud

conditioner el suavizante

condom el preservativo

conference la conferencia

confirm v confirmar

congestion la congestión

connect v (internet) conectarse

connection (internet) la conexión; ~ (flight) la conexión de vuelo

constipated estreñido

consulate el consulado

consultant el consultor

contact v ponerse en contacto con

contact lens la lentilla de contacto; **~ solution** el líquido de lentillas de contacto

contagious contagioso

convention hall el salón de congresos

conveyor belt la cinta transportadora

cook v cocinar

cooking gas el gas butano

cool (temperature) frío

copper el cobre

corkscrew el sacacorchos

cost v costar

cot el catre

cotton el algodón

cough v toser; ~ n la tos

country code el código de país

cover charge la entrada

crash v (car) estrellarse

cream (ointment) la pomada

credit card la tarjeta de crédito

crew neck el cuello redondo

crib la cuna

crystal el cristal

cup la taza

currency la moneda; **~ exchange** el cambio de divisas; **~ exchange office** la casa de cambio

current account [BE] la cuenta corriente

customs las aduanas

cut v (hair) cortar; ~ n (injury) el corte

cute mono

cycling el ciclismo

D

damage v causar daño

damaged ha sufrido daños

dance v bailar; **~ club** la discoteca

dangerous peligroso

dark oscuro

date (calendar) la fecha

day el día

deaf sordo

debit card la tarjeta de débito

deck chair la tumbona

declare v declarar

decline v (credit card) rechazar

deeply hondo

degrees (temperature) los grados

delay v retrasarse

delete v (computer) borrar

delicatessen la charcutería

delicious delicioso

denim tela vaquero

dentist el dentista

denture la dentadura

deodorant el desodorante

department store los grandes almacenes

departures (airport) las salidas

deposit v depositar; ~ n (bank) el depósito bancario; ~ v (reserve a room) la fianza

desert el desierto

dessert el postre

detergent el detergente

develop v (film) revelar

diabetic diabético

dial v marcar

diamond el diamante

diaper el pañal

diarrhea la diarrea

diesel el diesel

difficult difícil

digital digital; ~ camera la cámara digital; ~ photos las fotos digitales; ~ prints las fotos digitales

dining room el comedor

dinner la cena

direction la dirección

dirty sucio

disabled discapacitado; ~ accessible

[BE] el acceso para discapacitados

discharge (bodily fluid) la secreción

disconnect (computer) desconectar

discount el descuento

dish (kitchen) el plato; ~washer el lavavajillas; ~washing liquid el líquido lavavajillas

display v mostrar; ~ case la vitrina

disposable desechable; ~ razor la cuchilla desechable

dive v bucear

diving equipment el equipo de buceo

divorce v divorciar

dizzy mareado

doctor el médico

doll la muñeca

dollar (U.S.) el dólar

domestic nacional; ~ flight el vuelo nacional

door la puerta

dormitory el dormitorio

double bed la cama de matrimonio

downtown el centro

dozen la docena

drag lift el telesquí

dress (piece of clothing) el vestido; ~ code las normas de vestuario

drink v beber; ~ n la bebida; ~ menu la carta de bebidas;

~ing water el agua potable

drive v conducir

driver's license number el número de permiso de conducir

drop (medicine) la gota

drowsiness la somnolencia

dry cleaner la tintorería

dubbed doblada

during durante

duty (tax) el impuesto; ~-free libre de impuestos

DVD el DVD

E

ear la oreja; ~ache el dolor de oído

earlier más temprano

early temprano

earrings los pendientes

east el este

easy fácil

eat v comer

economy class la clase económica

elbow el codo

electric outlet el enchufe eléctrico

elevator el ascensor

e-mail v enviar un correo electrónico; ~ n el correo electrónico; ~ address la dirección de correo electrónico

emergency la emergencia; ~ exit la salida de urgencia

empty v vaciar

enamel (jewelry) el esmalte

end v terminar

English el inglés

engrave v grabar

enjoy v disfrutar

enter v entrar

entertainment el entretenimiento

entrance la entrada

envelope el sobre

equipment el equipo

escalators las escaleras mecánicas

e-ticket el billete electrónico

EU resident el/la residente de la UE

euro el euro

evening la noche

excess el exceso

exchange v (money) cambiar; ~ v (goods) devolver; ~ n (place) la casa de cambio; ~ rate el tipo de cambio

excursion la excursión

excuse v (to get past) pedir perdón; ~ v (to get attention) disculparse

exhausted agotado

exit v salir; ~ n la salida

expensive caro

expert (skill level) experto

exposure (film) la foto

express rápido; ~ bus el autobús rápido; ~ train el tren rápido

extension (phone) la extensión

extra adicional; **~ large** equis ele (XL)

extract v (tooth) extraer

eye el ojo

eyebrow wax la depilación de cejas

F

face la cara

facial la limpieza de cutis

family la familia

fan (appliance) el ventilador; **~ (souvenir)** el abanico

far lejos; **~-sighted** hipermétrope

farm la granja

fast rápido; **~ food** la comida rápida

faster más rápido

fat free sin grasa

father el padre

fax v enviar un fax; **~** n el fax; **~ number** el número de fax

fee la tasa

feed v alimentar

ferry el ferry

fever la fiebre

field (sports) el campo

fill v llenar ; **~ out** v (form) rellenar

filling (tooth) el empaste

film (camera) el carrete

fine (fee for breaking law) la multa

finger el dedo; **~nail** la uña del dedo

fire fuego; **~ department** los bomberos; **~ door** la puerta de incendios

first primero; **~ class** la primera clase

fit (clothing) quedar bien

fitting room el probador

fix v (repair) reparar

flashlight la linterna

flight el vuelo

floor el suelo

flower la flor

folk music la música folk

food la comida

foot el pie

football [BE] el fútbol

for para/por

forecast el pronóstico

forest el bosque

fork el tenedor

form el formulario

formula (baby) la fórmula infantil

fort el fuerte

fountain la fuente

free gratuito

freezer el congelador

fresh fresco

friend el amigo

frying pan la sartén

full completo; **~-service** el servicio completo; **~-time** a tiempo completo

G

game el partido

garage (parking) el garaje; **~ (repair)** el taller

garbage bag la bolsa de basura

gas la gasolina; **~ station** la gasolinera

gate (airport) la puerta

gay gay; **~ bar** el bar gay; **~ club** la discoteca gay

gel (hair) la gomina

get to v ir a

get off v (a train/bus/ subway) bajarse

gift el regalo; **~ shop** la tienda de regalos

girl la niña; **~friend** la novia

give v dar

glass (drinking) el vaso; **~ (material)** el vidrio

glasses las gafas

go v (somewhere) ir a

gold el oro

golf golf; **~ course** el campo de golf; **~ tournament** el torneo de golf

good n el producto; **~** adj bueno; **~ afternoon** buenas tardes; **~ evening** buenas noches; **~ morning** buenas días; **~bye** adiós

gram el gramo

grandchild el nieto

grandparent el abuelo

gray gris

green verde

grocery store el supermercado

ground la tierra; **~ floor** la planta baja; **~cloth** la tela impermeable

group el grupo

guide el guía; **~ book** la guía; **~ dog** el perro guía

gym el gimnasio

gynecologist el ginecólogo

H

hair el pelo; **~ dryer** el secador de pelo; **~ salon** la peluquería; **~brush** el cepillo de pelo; **~cut** el corte de pelo; **~spray** la laca; **~style** el peinado; **~stylist** el estilista

half medio; **~ hour** la media hora; **~-kilo** el medio kilo

hammer el martillo

hand la mano; **~ luggage [BE]** el equipaje de mano; **~bag [BE]** el bolso

handicapped discapacitado; **~-accessible** el acceso para discapacitados

hangover la resaca

happy feliz

hat el sombrero

have v tener

head (body part) la cabeza; **~ache** el dolor de cabeza; **~phones** los cascos
health la salud; **~ food store** la tienda de alimentos naturales
heart el corazón; **~ condition** padecer del corazón
heat v calentar; **~** n el calor
heater [heating BE] la calefacción
hello hola
helmet el casco
help v ayudar; **~** n la ayuda
here aquí
hi hola
high alto; **~chair** la trona; **~way** la autopista
hiking boots las botas de montaña
hill la colina
hire v [BE] alquilar; **~ car** [BE] el coche de alquiler
hitchhike v hacer autostop
hockey el hockey
holiday [BE] las vacaciones
horse track el hipódromo
hospital el hospital
hostel el albergue
hot (temperature) caliente; **~ (spicy)** picante; **~ spring** el agua termale; **~ water** el agua caliente
hotel el hotel
hour la hora
house la casa; **~hold goods** los artículos para el hogar; **~keeping services** el servicio de limpieza de habitaciones
how (question) cómo; **~ much (question)** cuánto cuesta
hug v abrazar
hungry hambriento
hurt v **(have pain)** tener dolor
husband el marido

I
ibuprofen el ibuprofeno
ice el hielo; **~ hockey** el hockey sobre hielo
icy adj helado
identification el documento de identidad
ill v **(to feel)** encontrarse mal
in dentro
include v incluir
indoor pool la piscina cubierta
inexpensive barato
infected infectado
information (phone) el número de teléfono de información; **~ desk** el mostrador de información
insect el insecto; **~ bite** la picadura de insecto; **~ repellent** el repelente de insectos
insert v introducir
insomnia el insomnio
instant message el mensaje instantáneo
insulin la insulina
insurance el seguro; **~ card** la tarjeta de seguro; **~ company** la compañía de seguros
interesting interesante
intermediate el nivel intermedio
international (airport area) internacional; **~ flight** el vuelo internacional; **~ student card** la tarjeta internacional de estudiante
internet la internet; **~ cafe** el cibercafé; **~ service** el servicio de internet; **wireless ~** el acceso inalámbrico
interpreter el/la intérprete
intersection el cruce
intestine el intestino
introduce v presentar
invoice [BE] la factura
Ireland Irlanda
Irish irlandés
iron v planchar; **~** n **(clothes)** la plancha
Italian italiano

J
jacket la chaqueta
jar el bote

jaw la mandíbula
jazz el jazz; **~ club** el club de jazz
jeans los vaqueros
jet ski la moto acuática
jeweler la joyería
jewelry las joyas
join v acompañar a
joint (body part) la articulación

K
key la llave; **~ card** la llave electrónica; **~ ring** el llavero
kiddie pool la piscina infantil
kidney (body part) el riñón
kilo el kilo; **~gram** el kilogramo; **~meter** el kilómetro
kiss v besar
kitchen la cocina; **~ foil** [BE] el papel de aluminio
knee la rodilla
knife el cuchillo

L
lace el encaje
lactose intolerant alérgico a la lactosa
lake el lago
large grande; **~er** más grande
last último
late (time) tarde; **~er** más tarde
launderette [BE] la lavandería
laundromat la lavandería

laundry la colada; **~ facility** la lavandería; **~ service** el servicio de lavandería

lawyer el abogado

leather el cuero

to leave v salir

left (direction) la izquierda

leg la pierna

lens la lente

less menos

lesson la lección

letter la carta

library la biblioteca

life la vida; **~ jacket** el chaleco salvavidas; **~guard** el socorrista

lift n el ascensor; **~** v **(to give a ride)** llevar en coche; **~ pass** el pase de acceso a los remontes

light n **(overhead)** la luz; **~** v **(cigarette)** dar fuego; **~bulb** la bombilla

lighter el mechero

like v gustar; **I like** me gusta

line (train) la línea

linen el lino

lip el labio

liquor store la tienda de bebidas alcohólicas

liter el litro

little pequeño

live v vivir

liver (body part) el hígado

loafers los mocasines

local de la zona

lock v cerrar; **~** n el cerrojo

locker la taquilla

log on v **(computer)** iniciar sesión

log off v **(computer)** cerrar sesión

long largo; **~ sleeves** las mangas largas; **~-sighted [BE]** hipermétrope

look v mirar

lose v **(something)** perder

lost perdido; **~ and found** la oficina de objetos perdidos

lotion la crema hidratante

louder más alto

love v querer; **~** n el amor

low bajo; **~er** más bajo

luggage el equipaje; **~ cart** el carrito de equipaje; **~ locker** la consigna automática; **~ ticket** el talón de equipaje; **hand ~ [BE]** el equipaje de mano

lunch la comida

lung el pulmón

M

magazine la revista

magnificent magnífico

mail v enviar por correo; **~** n el correo; **~box** el buzón de correo

main principal; **~ attractions** los principales sitios de interés; **~ course** el plato principal

make up a prescription v , **[BE]** despachar medicamentos

mall el centro comercial

man el hombre

manager el gerente

manicure la manicura

manual car el coche con transmisión manual

map el mapa

market el mercado

married casado

marry v casarse

mass (church service) la misa

massage el masaje

match la cerilla

meal la comida

measure v **(someone)** medir

measuring cup la taza medidora

measuring spoon la cuchara medidora

mechanic el mecánico

medicine el medicamento

medium (size) mediano

meet v **(someone)** conocer

meeting la reunión; **~ room** la sala de reuniones

membership card la tarjeta de socio

memorial (place) el monumento conmemorativo

memory card la tarjeta de memoria

mend v zurcir

menstrual cramps los dolores menstruales

menu la carta

message el mensaje

meter (parking) el parquímetro

microwave el microondas

midday [BE] el mediodía

midnight la medianoche

mileage el kilometraje

mini-bar el minibar

minute el minuto

missing desaparecido

mistake el error

mobile móvil; **~ home** la caravana; **~ phone [BE]** el teléfono móvil

mobility la movilidad

money el dinero

month el mes

mop la fregona

moped el ciclomotor

more más

morning la mañana

mosque la mezquita

mother la madre

motion sickness el mareo

motor el motor; **~ boat** la lancha motora; **~cycle** la motocicleta; **~way [BE]** la autopista

mountain la montaña;
~ **bike** la bicicleta
de montaña

mousse (hair) la
espuma para el pelo

mouth n la boca

movie la película; ~
theater el cine

mug v asaltar

muscle (body part) el
músculo

museum el museo

music la música; ~
store la tienda de
música

N

nail la u_na; ~ **file** la
lima de uñas; ~
salon el salon de
manicura

name el nombre

napkin la servilleta

nappy [BE] el pañale

nationality la
nacionalidad

nature preserve la
reserva natural

(be) nauseous v tener
náuseas

near cerca;
~**-sighted** miope;
~**by** cerca de aquí

neck el cuello

necklace el collar

need v necesitar

newspaper el
periódico

newsstand el quiosco

next próximo

nice adj amable

night la noche; ~**club**
la discoteca

no no

non sin; ~**-alco-
holic** sin alcohol;
~**-smoking** para no
fumadores

noon el mediodía

north el norte

nose la nariz

note [BE] el billete

nothing nada

notify v avisar

**novice (skill
level)** principiante

now ahora

number el número

nurse el enfermero/la
enfermera

O

office la oficina; ~
hours (doctor's) las
horas de consulta;
~ **hours (other of-
fices)** el horario de
oficina

off-licence [BE] la
tienda de bebidas
alcohólicas

oil el aceite

OK de acuerdo

old adj viejo

on the corner en la
esquina

once una vez

one uno; ~**-way
ticket** el billete
de ida; ~**-way
street** la calle de
sentido único

only solamente

open v abrir; ~ adj
abierto

opera la ópera; ~
house el teatro de
la ópera

opposite frente a

optician el oculista

orange (color) naranja

orchestra la orquesta

order v pedir

outdoor pool la
piscina exterior

outside fuera

over sobre; ~
**the counter
(medication)** sin
receta; ~**look
(scenic place)** el
mirador; ~**night** por
la noche

oxygen treatment
la oxigenoterapia

P

p.m. de la tarde

pacifier el chupete

pack v hacer las
maletas

package el paquete

paddling pool [BE] la
piscina infantil

pad [BE] la compresa

pain el dolor

pajamas los pijamas

palace el palacio

pants los pantalones

pantyhose las medias

paper el papel; ~
towel el papel de
cocina

paracetamol [BE] el
paracetamol

park v aparcar;
~ n el parque;
~**ing garage** el
párking; ~**ing lot** el
aparcamiento

**parliament build-
ing** el palacio de las

cortes

part (for car) la pieza;
~**time** a tiempo
parcial

pass through v estar
de paso

passenger el pasajero

passport el pasaporte;
~ **control** el control
de pasaportes

password la
contraseña

pastry shop la
pastelería

path el camino

pay v pagar; ~
phone el teléfono
público

**peak (of a moun-
tain)** la cima

pearl la perla

pedestrian el peatón

pediatrician el
pediatra

pedicure la pedicura

pen el bolígrafo

penicillin la penicilina

penis el pene

per por; ~ **day** por
día; ~ **hour** por
hora; ~ **night** por
noche; ~ **week** por
semana

perfume el perfume

period (menstrual) la
regla; ~ **(of time)** la
época

permit v permitir

petite las tallas
pequeñas

petrol la gasolina; ~
station la gaso-
linera

pewter el peltre

pharmacy la farmacia
phone v
hacer una llamada;
~ n el teléfono; ~
call la llamada de
teléfono; ~ **card** la
tarjeta telefónica; ~
number el número
de teléfono
photo la foto;
~**copy** la fotocopia;
~**graphy** la foto-
grafía
pick up v (some-
thing) recoger
picnic area la zona
para picnic
piece el trozo
Pill (birth control) la
píldora
pillow la almohada
**personal identifica-
tion number
(PIN)** la clave
pink rosa
piste [BE] la pista; ~
map [BE] el mapa
de pistas
pizzeria la pizzería
place v (a bet) hacer
una apuesta
plane el avión
plastic wrap el film
transparente
plate el plato
**platform [BE]
(train)** el andén
platinum el platino
play v jugar; ~ n
(theater) la obra de
teatro; ~**ground** el
patio de recreo;
~**pen** el parque
please por favor

pleasure el placer
plunger el desa-
tascador
plus size la talla
grande
pocket el bolsillo
poison el veneno
poles (skiing) los
bastones
police la policía; ~
report el certificado
de la policía; ~ **sta-
tion** la comisaría
pond el estanque
pool la piscina
pop music la música
pop
portion la ración
post [BE] el correo;
~ **office** la oficina
de correos; ~**box**
[BE] el buzón de
correos; ~**card** la
tarjeta postal
pot la olla
pottery la cerámica
**pounds (British
sterling)** las libras
esterlinas
pregnant embarazada
prescribe v recetar
prescription la receta
press v (cloth-
ing) planchar
price el precio
print v imprimir
problem el problema
produce las frutas y
verduras; ~ **store** la
frutería y verdulería
prohibit v prohibir
pronounce v
pronunciar
public el público

pull v (door sign) tirar
purple morado
purse el bolso
push v (door
sign) empujar;
~**chair [BE]** el
cochecito de niño

Q
quality n la calidad
question la pregunta
quiet adj tranquilo

R
racetrack el circuito
de carreras
racket (sports) la
raqueta
**railway station
[BE]** la estación de
trenes
rain la lluvia;
~**coat** el chubas-
quero; ~**forest** el
bosque pluvial;
~**y** adv lluvioso
rap (music) el rap
rape v violar; ~ n la
violación
rash la erupción
cutánea
razor blade la hoja de
afeitar
reach v localizar
ready listo
real auténtico
receipt el recibo
receive v recibir
reception la recepción
recharge v recargar
recommend v
recomendar
recommendation la
recomendación

recycle v reciclar
red rojo
refrigerator n la
nevera
region la región
registered mail el
correo certificado
regular normal
relationship la
relación
rent v alquilar
rental car el coche de
alquiler
repair v arreglar
repeat v repetir
reservation la
reserva;
~ **desk** la taquilla
reserve v reservar
restaurant el
restaurante
restroom el servicio
retired jubilado
return v (some-
thing) devolver; ~ n
[BE] la ida y vuelta
rib (body part) la
costilla
right (direction) derecha; ~ **of way** prior-
idad de paso
ring el anillo
river n el río
road map el mapa de
carreteras
rob v atracar
robbed atracado
romantic romántico
room la habitación;
~ **key** la llave de
habitación; ~ **ser-
vice** el servicio de
habitaciones
round-trip ida y vuelta

route la ruta
rowboat la barca de remos
rubbish [BE] la basura; ~ bag [BE] la bolsa de basura
rugby el rugby
ruins las ruinas
rush la prisa

S

sad triste
safe n la caja fuerte; ~ adj seguro
sales tax el IVA
same mismo
sandals las sandalias
sanitary napkin la compresa
saucepan el cazo
sauna la sauna
save v (computer) guardar
savings (account) la cuenta de ahorro
scanner el escáner
scarf la bufanda
schedule v programar; ~ n el horario
school el colegio
science la ciencia
scissors las tijeras
sea el mar
seat el asiento
security la seguridad
see v ver
self-service el autoservicio
sell v vender
seminar el seminario
send v enviar
senior citizen jubilado
separated (marriage) -separado

serious serio
service (in a restaurant) el servicio
sexually transmitted disease (STD) la enfermedad de transmisión sexual
shampoo el champú
sharp afilado
shaving cream la crema de afeitar
sheet la sábana
ship v enviar
shirt la camisa
shoe store la zapatería
shoes los zapatos
shop v comprar
shopping ir de compras; ~ area la zona de compras; ~ centre [BE] el centro comercial; ~ mall el centro comercial
short corto; ~ sleeves las mangas cortas; ~s los pantalones cortos; ~-sighted [BE] miope
shoulder el hombro
show v enseñar
shower la ducha
shrine el santuario
sick enfermo
side el lado; ~ dish la guarnición; ~ effect el efecto secundario; ~ order la guarnición
sightsee v hacer turismo
sightseeing tour el recorrido turístico

sign v (name) firmar
silk la seda
silver la plata
single (unmarried) soltero; ~ bed la cama; ~ prints una copia; ~ room una habitación individual
sink el lavabo
sister la hermana
sit v sentarse
size la talla
skin la piel
skirt la falda
ski v esquiar; ~ n el esquí; ~ lift el telesquí
sleep v dormir; ~er car el coche cama; ~ing bag el saco de dormir
slice v cortar en rodajas
slippers las zapatillas
slower más despacio
slowly despacio
small pequeño
smaller más pequeño
smoke v fumar
smoking (area) la zona de fumadores
snack bar la cafetería
sneakers las zapatillas de deporte
snorkeling equipment el equipo de esnórquel
snow la nieve; ~board la tabla de snowboard; ~shoe la raqueta de nieve; ~y nevado
soap el jabón

soccer el fútbol
sock el calcetín
some alguno
soother [BE] el chupete
sore throat las anginas
sorry lo siento
south el sur
souvenir el recuerdo; ~ store la tienda de recuerdos
spa el centro de salud y belleza
Spain España
Spanish el español
spatula la espátula
speak v hablar
special (food) la especialidad de la casa
specialist (doctor) el especialista
specimen el ejemplar
speeding el exceso de velocidad
spell v deletrear
spicy picante
spine (body part) la columna vertebral
spoon la cuchara
sports los deportes; ~ massage el masaje deportivo
sporting goods store la tienda de deportes
sprain el esguince
square cuadrado; ~ kilometer el kilómetro cuadrado; ~ meter el metro cuadrado
stadium el estadio

stairs las escaleras
stamp v **(a ticket)** picar; ~ n **(postage)** el sello
start v empezar
starter [BE] el aperitivo
station la estación; **bus** ~ la estación de autobuses; **gas** ~ la gasolinera; **muster** ~ **[BE]** el punto de reunión; **petrol** ~ **[BE]** la gasolinera; **subway** ~ el metro; **train** ~ la estación de tren
statue la estatua
stay v quedarse
steal v robar
steep empinado
sterling silver la plata esterlina
sting el escozor
stolen robado
stomach el estómago; ~**ache** el dolor de estómago
stop v pararse; ~ n la parada
storey [BE] la planta
stove el horno
straight recto
strange extraño
stream el arroyo
stroller el cochecito
student el estudiante
study v estudiar
stunning impresionante
subtitle el subtítulo
subway el metro; ~ **station** la estación

de metro
suit el traje
suitcase la maleta
sun el sol; ~**block** el protector solar total; ~**burn** la quemadura solar; ~**glasses** las gafas de sol; ~**ny** soleado; ~**screen** el protector solar; ~**stroke** la insolación
super (fuel) súper; ~**market** el supermercado
surfboard la tabla de surf
surgical spirit [BE] el alcohol etílico
swallow v tragar
sweater el jersey
sweatshirt la sudadera
sweet (taste) dulce; ~**s [BE]** los caramelos
swelling la hinchazón
swim v nadar; ~**suit** el bañador
symbol (keyboard) el símbolo
synagogue la sinagoga

T

table la mesa
tablet (medicine) el comprimido
take v llevar; ~ **away [BE]** para llevar
tampon el tampón
tapas bar el bar de tapas
taste v probar

taxi el taxi
team el equipo
telephone el teléfono
temporary provisional
tennis el tenis
tent la tienda de campaña; ~ **peg** la estaca; ~ **pole** el mástil
terminal (airport) el terminal
terracotta la terracota
terrible terrible
text v **(send a message)** enviar un mensaje de texto; ~ n **(message)** el texto
thank v dar las gracias a; ~ **you** gracias
that eso
theater el teatro
there ahí
thief el ladrón
thigh el muslo
thirsty sediento
this esto
throat la garganta
ticket el billete; ~ **office** el despacho de billetes; ~**ed passenger** el pasajero con billete
tie (clothing) la corbata
time el tiempo; ~**table [BE]** el horario
tire la rueda
tired cansado
tissue el pañuelo de papel
tobacconist el estanco

today hoy
toe el dedo del pie; ~**nail** la uña del pie
toilet [BE] el servicio; ~ **paper** el papel higiénico
tomorrow mañana
tongue la lengua
tonight esta noche
too demasiado
tooth el diente; ~**brush** el cepillo de dientes; ~**paste** la pasta de dientes
total (amount) el total
tough (food) duro
tourist el turista; ~ **information office** la oficina de turismo
tour el recorrido turístico
tow truck la grúa
towel la toalla
tower la torre
town la ciudad; ~ **hall** el ayuntamiento; ~ **map** el mapa de ciudad; ~ **square** la plaza
toy el juguete; ~ **store** la tienda de juguetes
track (train) el andén
traditional tradicional
traffic light el semáforo
trail la pista; ~ **map** el mapa de la pista
trailer el remolque
train el tren; ~ **station** la estación de tren

transfer v cambiar
translate v traducir
trash la basura
travel v viajar; **~ agency** la agencia de viajes; **~ sickness** el mareo; **~er's check [cheque BE]** el cheque de viaje
tree el árbol
trim (hair cut) cortarse las puntas
trip el viaje
trolley [BE] el carrito
trousers [BE] los pantalones
T-shirt la camiseta
turn off v apagar
turn on v encender
TV la televisión
type v escribir a máquina
tyre [BE] la rueda

U

United Kingdom (U.K.) el Reino Unido
United States (U.S.) los Estados Unidos
ugly feo
umbrella el paraguas
unattended desatendido
unconscious inconsciente
underground [BE] el metro; **~ station [BE]** la estación de metro
underpants [BE] los calzoncillos

understand v entender
underwear la ropa interior
university la universidad
unleaded (gas) la gasolina sin plomo
upper superior
urgent urgente
use v usar
username el nombre de usuario
utensil el cubierto

V

vacancy la habitación libre
vacation las vacaciones
vaccination la vacuna
vacuum cleaner la aspiradora
vaginal infection la infección vaginal
valid validez
valley el valle
valuable valioso
VAT [BE] el IVA
vegetarian vegetariano
vehicle registration el registro del coche
viewpoint [BE] el mirador
village el pueblo
vineyard la viña
visa (passport document) el visado
visit v visitar; **~ing hours** el horario de visita
visually impaired la persona con

discapacidad visual
vitamin la vitamina
V-neck el cuello de pico
vomit v vomitar

W

wait v esperar; **~** n la espera; **~ing room** la sala de espera
waiter el camarero
waitress la camarera
wake v despertarse; **~-up call** la llamada despertador
walk v caminar; **~** n la caminata; **~ing route** la ruta de senderismo
wallet la cartera
warm v (something) calentar; **~** adj (temperature) calor
washing machine la lavadora
watch el reloj
waterfall la cascada
weather el tiempo
week la semana; **~end** el fin de semana; **~ly** semanal
welcome v acoger
well bien; **~-rested** descansado
west el oeste
what (question) qué
wheelchair la silla de ruedas; **~ ramp** la rampa para silla de ruedas
when (question) cuándo

where (question) dónde
white blanco; **~ gold** el oro blanco
who (question) quién
widowed viudo
wife la mujer
window la ventana; **~ case** el escaparate
windsurfer el surfista
wine list la carta de vinos
wireless inalámbrico; **~ internet** el acceso inalámbrico a internet; **~ internet service** el servicio inalámbrico a internet; **~ phone** el teléfono móvil
with con
withdraw v retirar; **~al (bank)** retirar fondos
without sin
woman la mujer
wool la lana
work v trabajar
wrap v envolver
wrist la muñeca
write v escribir

Y

year el año
yellow amarillo
yes sí
yesterday ayer
young joven
youth hostel el albergue juvenil

Z

zoo el zoológico

SPANISH–ENGLISH

A

a tiempo completo full-time

a tiempo parcial part-time

la abadía abbey

el abanico fan (souvenir)

abierto *adj* open

el abogado lawyer

abrazar *v* hug

el abrebotellas bottle opener

el abrelatas can opener

el abrigo coat

abrir *v* open

el abuelo grandparent

aburrido boring

acampar *v* camp

el acantilado cliff

el acceso access; ~ **inalámbrico a internet** wireless internet; ~ **para discapacitados** handicapped- [disabled-BE] accessible

el accidente accident

el aceite oil

aceptar *v* accept

acoger *v* welcome

acompañar a *v* join

la acupuntura acupuncture

el adaptador adapter

adicional extra

adiós goodbye

las aduanas customs

el aeropuerto airport

afilado sharp

la agencia agency; ~ **de viajes** travel agency

agotado exhausted

el agua water; ~ **caliente** hot water; ~ **potable** drinking water

las aguas termales hot spring

ahí there

ahora now

el aire air, air pump; ~ **acondicionado** air conditioning

el albergue hostel; ~ **juvenil** youth hostel

alérgico allergic; ~ **a la lactosa** lactose intolerant

algo anything

el algodón cotton

alguno some

alimentar *v* feed

el allanamiento de morada break-in (burglary)

la almohada pillow

el alojamiento accommodation

alquilar *v* rent (hire BE); **el** ~ **de coches** car rental (hire BE)

alto high

amable nice

amarillo yellow

la ambulancia ambulance

el amigo friend

el amor *n* love

el andén track [platform BE] (train)

anémico anemic

la anestesia anesthesia

las anginas sore throat

el anillo ring

el animal animal

antes de before

el antibiótico antibiotic

el año year

apagar *v* turn off

el aparcamiento parking lot [car park BE]

aparcar *v* park

el apartamento apartment

el apéndice appendix (body part)

el aperitivo appetizer [starter BE]

aquí here

el árbol tree

la aromaterapia aromatherapy

arreglar *v* repair

el arroyo stream

la arteria artery

la articulación joint (body part)

los artículos goods; ~ **para el hogar** household good

la artritis arthritis

asaltar *v* mug

el asalto attack

el ascensor elevator [lift BE]

asiático Asian

el asiento seat; ~ **de niño** car seat; ~ **de pasillo** aisle seat

asistir *v* attend

asmático asthmatic

la aspiradora vacuum cleaner

la aspirina aspirin

atracado robbed

atracar *v* rob

Australia Australia

australiano Australian

auténtico real

el autobús bus; ~ **rápido** express bus

automático automatic

la autopista highway [motorway BE]

el autoservicio self-service

la avería breakdown

el avión airplane, plane

avisar *v* notify

ayer yesterday

la ayuda *n* help

ayudar *v* help

el ayuntamiento town hall

azul blue

B

bailar *v* dance

bajarse *v* get off (a train, bus, subway)

bajo low

el ballet ballet

el baloncesto basketball

el bálsamo para después del afeitado aftershave

el banco bank

el bañador swimsuit

el baño bathroom

el bar bar; **~ de tapas** tapas bar; **~ gay** gay bar

barato cheap, inexpensive

la barbacoa barbecue

la barca de remos rowboat

el barco boat

los bastones poles (skiing)

la basura trash [rubbish BE]

la batería battery (car)

el bebé baby

beber v drink

la bebida n drink

beis beige

el béisbol baseball

besar v kiss

el biberón baby bottle

la biblioteca library

la bicicleta bicycle; **~ de montaña** mountain bike

el billete n bill (money); **~ de autobús** bus ticket; **~ de ida** one-way (ticket); **~ de ida y vuelta** round trip [return BE]; **~ electrónico** e-ticket

el biquini bikini

blanco white

la blusa blouse

la boca mouth

el bolígrafo pen

la bolsa de basura garbage [rubbish BE] bag

el bolsillo pocket

el bolso purse [handbag BE]

los bomberos fire department

la bombilla lightbulb

borrar v clear (on an ATM); **~** v delete (computer)

el bosque forest; **~ pluvial** rainforest

las botas boots; **~ de montaña** hiking boots

el bote jar

la botella bottle

el brazo arm

británico British

el broche brooch

bucear to dive

bueno adj good

buenas noches good evening

buenas tardes good afternoon

buenos días good morning

la bufanda scarf

el buzón de correo mailbox [postbox BE]

C

la cabaña cabin (house)

el cabaré cabaret

la cabeza head (body part)

la cafetería cafe, coffee shop, snack bar

la caja case (amount); **~ fuerte** n safe

el cajero cashier; **~ automático** ATM

el calcetín sock

la calefacción heater [heating BE]

calentar v heat, warm

la calidad quality

la calle de sentido único one-way street

calor hot, warm (temperature)

las calorías calories

los calzoncillos briefs [underpants BE] (clothing)

la cama single bed; **~ de matrimonio** double bed

la cámara camera; **~ digital** digital camera

la camarera waitress

el camarero waiter

el camarote cabin (ship)

cambiar v change, exchange, transfer

el cambio n change (money); **~ de divisas** currency exchange

caminar v walk

la caminata n walk

el camino path

la camisa shirt

la camiseta T-shirt

el cámping campsite

el campo field (sports); **~ de batalla** battleground; **~ de golf** golf course

Canadá Canada

canadiense Canadian

cancelar v cancel

el/la canguro babysitter

cansado tired

el cañón canyon

la cara face

los caramelos candy [sweets BE]

la caravana mobile home

el carbón charcoal

el carnicero butcher

caro expensive

el carrete film (camera)

el carrito cart [trolley BE] (grocery store); **~ de equipaje** luggage cart

la carta letter

la carta n menu; **~ de bebidas** drink menu; **~ para niños** children's menu; **~ de vinos** wine list

la cartera n wallet

el cartón carton; **~ de tabaco** carton of cigarettes

la casa house; **~ de cambio** currency exchange office

casado married

casarse v marry

la cascada waterfall

el casco helmet

los cascos headphones
el casino casino
el castillo castle
el catarro cold (sickness)
la catedral cathedral
el catre cot
causar daño *v* damage
el cazo saucepan
el CD CD
la cena dinner
el centímetro centimeter
el centro downtown area; **~ comercial** shopping mall [centre BE]; **~ de negocios** business center; **~ de salud y belleza** spa
el cepillo de pelo hair brush
la cerámica pottery
cerca near; **~ de aquí** nearby
la cerilla *n* match
cerrado closed
cerrar *v* close, lock; **~ sesión** *v* log off (computer)
el cerrojo *n* lock
el certificado certificate; **~ de la policía** police report
la cesta basket (grocery store)
el chaleco salvavidas life jacket
el champú shampoo
la chaqueta jacket
la charcutería delicatessen

el cheque *n* check [cheque BE] (payment); **~ de viaje** traveler's check [cheque BE]
el chicle chewing gum
chino Chinese
el chubasquero raincoat
el chupete pacifier [soother BE]
el cibercafé internet cafe
el ciclismo cycling
el ciclomotor moped
la ciencia science
el cigarrillo cigarette
la cima peak (of a mountain)
el cine movie theater
la cinta transportadora conveyor belt
el cinturón *n* belt
el circuito de carreras racetrack
la cita appointment
la ciudad town
la clase class; **~ económica** economy class; **~ preferente** business class
la clave personal identification number (PIN)
el club de jazz jazz club
cobrar *v* bill (charge); **~** *v* cash; **~** *v* charge (credit card)
el cobre copper
el coche *n* car; **~ de alquiler** rental (hire BE) car; **~ automático**

automatic car; **~ cama** sleeper [sleeping BE] car; **~ con transmisión manual** manual car
el cochecito stroller [pushchair BE]
la cocina kitchen
cocinar *v* cook
el código de país country code
el codo elbow
la colada laundry
el colegio school
la colina hill
el collar necklace
la colonia cologne
el color color
la columna vertebral spine (body part)
el comedor dining room
comer *v* eat
la comida food, lunch, meal; **~ rápida** fast food
la comisaría police station
cómo how
el compañero de trabajo colleague
la compañía company; **~ aérea** airline; **~ de seguros** insurance company
comprar *v* buy, shop
la compresa sanitary napkin [pad BE]
el comprimido tablet (medicine)
con with; **~ plomo** leaded (gas)
el concierto concert

conducir *v* drive
conectarse *v* connect (internet)
la conexión connection (internet); **~ de vuelo** connection (flight)
la conferencia conference
confirmar *v* confirm
el congelador freezer
la congestión congestion
conocer *v* meet (someone)
la consigna automática luggage locker
el consulado Consulate
el consultor consultant
contagioso contagious
la contraseña password
el control de pasaportes passport control
el corazón heart
la corbata tie (clothing)
el correo *n* mail [post BE]; **~ aéreo** airmail; **~ certificado** registered mail; **~ electrónico** *n* e-mail
cortar *v* cut (hair); **~ en rodajas** to slice
cortarse las puntas *v* trim (hair cut)
el corte *n* cut (injury); **~ de pelo** haircut
corto short

costar v cost

la costilla rib (body part)

la crema cream; **~ antiséptica** antiseptic cream; **~ de afeitar** shaving cream; **~ hidratante** lotion

el cristal crystal

el cruce intersection

cuándo when (question)

cuánto cuesta how much

el cubierto utensil

la cuchara spoon; **~ medidora** measuring spoon

la cucharadita teaspoon

la cuchilla desechable disposable razor

el cuchillo knife

el cuello neck; **~ de pico** V-neck; **~ redondo** crew neck

el cuenco bowl

la cuenta account; **~ de ahorro** savings account; **~ corriente** checking (current BE) account

cuero leather

la cueva cave

el cumpleaños birthday

la cuna crib

D

dar to give; **~ el pecho** breastfeed; **~ fuego** light (cigarette); **~ las gracias a** v thank

de from, of; **~ acuerdo** OK; **~ la mañana** a.m.; **~ la tarde** p.m.; **~ la zona** local

declarar v declare

el dedo finger; **~ del pie** toe

deletrear v spell

delicioso delicious

la dentadura denture

el dentista dentist

dentro in

la depilacion wax; **~ de cejas** eyebrow wax; **~ de las ingles** bikini wax

deportes sports

depositar v deposit

el depósito bancario deposit (bank)

la derecha right (direction)

desaparecido missing

el desatascador plunger

desatendido unattended

el desayuno breakfast

descansado well-rested

desconectar v disconnect (computer)

el descuento discount

desechable disposable

el desierto desert

el desodorante deodorant

despachar medicamentos v fill (make up BE) a prescription

el despacho de billetes ticket office

despacio slowly

despertarse v wake

después after

el detergente detergent

detrás de behind (direction)

devolver v exchange, return (goods)

el día day

diabético diabetic

el diamante diamond

la diarrea diarrhea

el diente tooth

el diesel diesel

difícil difficult

digital digital

el dinero money

la dirección direction

la dirección address; **~ de correo electrónico** e-mail address

discapacitado handicapped (disabled BE)

la discoteca club (dance, night); **~ gay** gay club

disculparse v excuse (to get attention)

disfrutar v enjoy

disponible available

divorciar v divorce

doblada dubbed

doblando (la esquina) around (the corner)

la docena dozen

el documento de identidad identification

el dólar dollar (U.S.)

el dolor pain; **~ de cabeza** headache; **~ de espalda** backache; **~ de estómago** stomachache; **~ de oído** earache; **~ de pecho** chest pain

los dolores menstruales menstrual cramps

dónde where (question)

dormir v sleep

el dormitorio dormitory

la ducha shower

dulce sweet (taste)

durante during

el DVD DVD

E

la edad age

el edificio building

el efectivo cash

el efecto secundario side effect

el ejemplar specimen

embarazada pregnant

embarcar v board

la emergencia emergency

el empaste filling (tooth)

empezar v begin, start

empinado steep

empujar v push (door sign)

en la esquina on the corner

el encaje lace

encender v turn on

el enchufe eléctrico electric outlet

encontrarse mal *v* be ill

la enfermedad de transmisión sexual sexually transmitted disease (STD)

el enfermero/la enfermera nurse

enfermo sick

enseñar *v* show

entender *v* understand

la entrada admission/cover charge; **~ entrance**

entrar *v* enter

el entretenimiento entertainment

enviar *v* send, ship; **~ por correo** *v* mail; **~ un correo electrónico** *v* e-mail; **~ un fax** *v* fax; **~ un mensaje de texto** *v* text (send a message)

envolver *v* wrap

la época period (of time)

el equipaje luggage [baggage BE]; **~ de mano** carry-on (piece of hand luggage)

el equipo team

el equipo equipment; **~ de buceo** diving equipment; **~ de esnórquel** snorkeling equipment

equis ele (XL) extra large

el error mistake

la erupción cutánea rash

las escaleras stairs; **~ mecánicas** escalators

el escáner scanner

el escaparate window case

la escoba broom

el escozor sting

escribir *v* write; **~ a máquina** *v* type

el escurridor colander

el esguince sprain

el esmalte enamel (jewelry)

eso that

la espalda back

España Spain

el español Spanish

la espátula spatula

la especialidad de la casa special (food)

el especialista specialist (doctor)

la espera *n* wait

esperar *v* wait

la espuma para el pelo mousse (hair)

el esquí *n* ski

esquiar *v* ski

los esquís acuáticos water skis

esta noche tonight

la estaca tent peg

la estación station; **~ de autobuses** bus station; **~ de metro** subway [underground BE] station; **~ de tren** train [railway BE] station

el estadio stadium

el estado de salud condition (medical)

los Estados Unidos United States (U.S.)

estadounidense American

el estanco tobacconist

el estanque pond

estar *v* be; **~ de paso** *v* pass through

la estatua statue

el este east

el estilista hairstylist

esto this

el estómago stomach

estrellarse *v* crash (car)

estreñido constipated

estudiando studying

el estudiante student

estudiar *v* study

el euro euro

el exceso excess; **~ de velocidad** speeding

la excursión excursion

experto expert (skill level)

la extensión extension (phone)

extraer *v* extract (tooth)

extraño strange

F

fácil *adj* easy

la factura bill (invoice BE)

la facturación check-in (airport)

facturar check (luggage)

la falda skirt

la familia family

el fax *n* fax

la fecha date (calendar)

feliz *adj* happy

feo *adj* ugly

el ferry ferry

la fianza deposit (to reserve a room)

la fiebre fever

el film transparente plastic wrap [cling film BE]

el fin de semana weekend

firmar *v* sign (name)

la flor flower

la fórmula infantil formula (baby)

el formulario form

la foto exposure (film); **~ photo**; **~copia** photocopy; **~grafía** photography; **~ digital** digital photo

la fregona mop

los frenos brakes (car)

frente a opposite

fresco fresh

frío *adj* cold (temperature)

las frutas y verduras produce

la frutería y verdulería produce store

el fuego fire

la fuente fountain

fuera outside

el fuerte fort

fumar *v* smoke

la funda para la cámara camera case
el fútbol soccer [football BE]

G

las gafas glasses; ~ de sol sunglasses
el garaje garage (parking)
la garganta throat
la garrafa carafe
el gas butano cooking gas
la gasolina gas [petrol BE]; ~ sin plomo unleaded gas
la gasolinera gas [petrol BE] station
gay gay
el gerente manager
el gimnasio gym
el ginecólogo gynecologist
la gomina gel (hair)
la gota drop (medicine)
grabar v burn (CD); ~ v engrave
gracias thank you
los grados degrees (temperature); ~ centígrado Celsius
el gramo gram
grande large
los grandes almacenes department store
la granja farm
gratuito free
gris gray
la grúa tow truck
el grupo group
guapo attractive

guardar v save (computer)
la guarnición side dish, order
el guía guide
la guía guide book; ~ de tiendas store directory
gustar v like; me gusta I like

H

ha sufrido daños damaged
la habitación room; ~ individual single room; ~ libre vacancy
hablar v speak
hacer v have; ~ una apuesta v place (a bet); ~ un arreglo v alter; ~ una llamada v phone; ~ las maletas v pack; ~ turismo sightseeing
hambriento hungry
helado icy
la hermana sister
el hermano brother
el hielo ice
el hígado liver (body part)
la hinchazón swelling
hipermétrope far-sighted [long-sighted BE]
el hipódromo horse-track
el hockey hockey; ~ sobre hielo ice hockey
la hoja de afeitar ra-

zor blade
hola hello
el hombre man
el hombro shoulder
hondo deeply
la hora hour
el horario n schedule [timetable BE]
los horarios hours; ~ de atención al público business hours; ~ de oficina office hours; ~ de visita visiting hours
las horas de consulta office hours (doctor's)
el hornillo camp stove
el horno stove
el hospital hospital
el hotel hotel
hoy today
el hueso bone

I

el ibuprofeno ibuprofen
la ida y vuelta round-trip [return BE]
la iglesia church
impresionante stunning
imprimir v print
el impuesto duty (tax)
incluir v include
inconsciente unconscious
increíble amazing
la infección vaginal vaginal infection
infectado infected
el inglés English

iniciar sesión v log on (computer)
el insecto bug
la insolación sunstroke
el insomnio insomnia
la insulina insulin
interesante interesting
internacional international (airport area)
la internet internet
el/la intérprete interpreter
el intestino intestine
introducir v insert
ir a v go (somewhere)
ir de compras v go shopping
Irlanda Ireland
irlandés Irish
el IVA sales tax [VAT BE]
la izquierda left (direction)

J

el jabón soap
el jardín botánico botanical garden
el jazz jazz
el jersey sweater
joven young
las joyas jewelry
la joyería jeweler
jubilado retired
jugar v play
el juguete toy

K

el kilo kilo; ~gramo kilogram; ~metraje mileage

el kilómetro kilometer; **~ cuadrado** square kilometer

L

el labio lip
la laca hairspray
el ladrón thief
el lago lake
la lana wool
la lancha motora motor boat
largo long
el lavabo sink
la lavadora washing machine
la lavandería laundromat [launderette BE]
lavar v wash
el lavavajillas dishwasher
la lección lesson
lejos far
la lengua tongue
la lente lens
las lentillas de contacto contact lens
las letras arts
las libras esterlinas pounds (British sterling)
libre de impuestos duty-free
la librería bookstore
el libro book
la lima de uñas nail file
limpiar v clean
la limpieza de cutis facial
limpio adj clean
la línea line (train)
el lino linen
la linterna flashlight

el líquido liquid; **~ de lentillas de contacto** contact lens solution; **~ lavavajillas** dishwashing liquid
listo ready
la litera berth
el litro liter
la llamada n call; **~ de teléfono** phone call; **~ despertador** wake-up call
llamar v call
la llave key; **~ de habitación** room key; **~ electrónica** key card
el llavero key ring
las llegadas arrivals (airport)
llegar v arrive
llenar v fill
llevar v take; **~ en coche** lift (to give a ride)
la lluvia rain
lluvioso rainy
lo siento sorry
localizar v reach
la luz light (overhead)

M

la madre mother
magnífico magnificent
el malestar estomacal upset stomach
la maleta bag, suitcase
la mandíbula jaw
las mangas cortas short sleeves
las mangas lar-

gas long sleeves
la manicura manicure
la mano hand
la manta blanket
mañana tomorrow; **la ~** morning
el mapa map; **~ de carreteras** road map; **~ de ciudad** town map; **~ de la pista** trail [piste BE] map
el mar sea
marcar v dial
mareado dizzy
el mareo motion [travel] sickness
el marido husband
marrón brown
el martillo hammer
más more; **~ alto** louder; **~ bajo** lower; **~ barato** cheaper; **~ despacio** slower; **~ grande** larger; **~ pequeño** smaller; **~ rápido** faster; **~ tarde** later; **~ temprano** earlier
el masaje massage; **~ deportivo** sports massage
el mástil tent pole
el mecánico mechanic
el mechero lighter
la media hora half hour
mediano medium (size)
la medianoche midnight
el medicamento medicine

el médico doctor
medio half; **~ kilo** half-kilo; **~día** noon [midday BE]
medir v measure (someone)
mejor best
menos less
el mensaje message; **~ instantáneo** instant message
el mercado market
el mes month
la mesa table
el metro subway [underground BE]
el metro cuadrado square meter
la mezquita mosque
el microondas microwave
el minibar mini-bar
el minuto minute
el mirador overlook [viewpoint BE] (scenic place)
mirar v look
la misa mass (church service)
mismo same
los mocasines loafers
la mochila backpack
molestar v bother
la moneda coin, currency
mono cute
la montaña n mountain
el monumento conmemorativo memorial (place)
morado purple

el mostrador de información information desk

mostrar v display

la moto acuática jet ski

la motocicleta motorcycle

movilidad mobility

la mujer wife, woman

la multa fine (fee for breaking law)

la muñeca doll; ~ wrist

el músculo muscle

el museo museum

la música music; ~ clásica classical music; ~ folk folk music; ~ pop pop music

el muslo thigh

N

nacional domestic

la nacionalidad nationality

nada nothing

nadar v swim

las nalgas buttocks

naranja orange (color)

la nariz nose

necesitar v need

los negocios business

negro black

nevado snowy

la nevera refrigerator

el nieto grandchild

la niña girl

el niño boy, child

el nivel intermedio intermediate

no no

la noche evening,

night

el nombre name; ~ de usuario username

normal regular

las normas de vestuario dress code

el norte north

la novia girlfriend

el novio boyfriend

el número number; ~ de fax fax number; ~ de permiso de conducir driver's license number; ~ de teléfono phone number; ~ de teléfono de información information (phone)

O

la obra de teatro n play (theater)

el oculista optician

el oeste west

la oficina office; ~ de correos post office; ~ de objetos perdidos lost and found; ~ de turismo tourist information office

el ojo eye

la olla pot

la ópera opera

el ordenador computer

la oreja ear

la orina urine

el oro gold; ~ amarillo yellow gold; ~ blanco white gold

la orquesta orchestra

oscuro dark

el otro camino alternate route

la oxigenoterapia oxygen treatment

P

padecer del corazón heart condition

el padre father

pagar v pay

el pájaro bird

el palacio palace; ~ de las cortes parliament building

los palillos chinos chopsticks

la panadería bakery

los pantalones pants [trousers BE]; ~ cortos shorts

el pañal diaper [nappy BE]

el pañuelo de paper tissue

el papel paper; ~ de aluminio aluminum [kitchen BE] foil; ~ de cocina paper towel; ~ higiénico toilet paper

el paquete package

para for; ~ llevar to go [take away BE]; ~ no fumadores non-smoking

el paracetamol acetaminophen [paracetamol BE]

la parada n stop; ~ de autobús bus stop

el paraguas umbrella

pararse v stop

el párking parking garage

el parque playpen; ~ park; ~ de atracciones amusement park

el partido game; ~ de fútbol soccer [football BE]; ~ de voleibol volleyball game

el pasajero passenger; ~ con billete ticketed passenger

el pasaporte passport

el pase de acceso a los remontes lift pass

el pasillo aisle

la pasta de dientes toothpaste

la pastelería pastry shop

el patio de recreo playground

el peatón pedestrian

el pecho chest (body part)

el pediatra pediatrician

la pedicura pedicure

pedir v order

el peinado hairstyle

el peine comb

la película movie

peligroso dangerous

el pelo hair

el peltre pewter

la peluquería de caballeros barber

la peluquería hair salon

los pendientes earrings

el pene penis

la penicilina penicillin

la pensión bed and breakfast

pequeño small

perder *v* lose (something)

perdido lost

el perfume perfume

el periódico newspaper

la perla pearl

permitir *v* allow, permit

el perro guía guide dog

la persona con discapacidad visual visually impaired person

la picadura de insecto insect bite

picante spicy

picar *v* stamp (a ticket)

el pie foot

la piel skin

la pierna leg

la pieza part (for car)

los pijamas pajamas

la pila battery

la píldora Pill (birth control)

la piscina pool; ~ **cubierta** indoor pool; ~ **exterior** outdoor pool; ~ **infantil** kiddie [paddling BE] pool

la pista trail [piste BE]

la pizzería pizzeria

el placer pleasure

la plancha *n* iron (clothes)

planchar *v* iron

la planta floor [storey BE]; ~ **baja** ground floor

la plata silver; ~ **esterlina** sterling silver

el platino platinum

el plato dish (kitchen); ~ **principal** main course

la playa beach

la plaza town square

la policía police

la pomada cream (ointment)

ponerse en contacto con *v* contact

por for; ~ per; ~ **día** per day; ~ **favor** please; ~ **hora** per hour; ~ **la noche** overnight; ~ **noche** per night; ~ **semana** per week

el postre dessert

el precio price

precioso beautiful

el prefijo area code

la pregunta question

presentar *v* introduce

el preservativo condom

la primera clase first class

primero first

los principales sitios de interés main attraction

principiante beginner, novice (skill level)

la prioridad de paso right of way

la prisa rush

el probador fitting room

probar *v* taste

el problema problem

el producto good; ~ **de limpieza** cleaning product

programar *v* schedule

prohibir *v* prohibit

el pronóstico forecast

pronunciar *v* pronounce

el protector solar sunscreen

provisional temporary

próximo next

el público public

el pueblo village

el puente bridge

la puerta gate (airport); ~ door; ~ **de incendios** fire door

el pulmón lung

la pulsera bracelet

el puro cigar

Q

qué what (question)

quedar bien *v* fit (clothing)

quedarse *v* stay

la queja complaint

la quemadura solar sunburn

querer *v* love (someone)

quién who (question)

el quiosco newsstand

R

la ración portion; ~ **para niños** children's portion

la rampa para silla de ruedas wheelchair ramp

el rap rap (music)

rápido express, fast

la raqueta racket (sports); ~ **de nieve** snowshoe

la reacción alérgica allergic reaction

recargar *v* recharge

la recepción reception

la receta prescription

recetar *v* prescribe

rechazar *v* decline (credit card)

recibir *v* receive

el recibo receipt

reciclar recycling

recoger *v* pick up (something)

la recogida de equipajes baggage claim

la recomendación recommendation

recomendar *v* recommend

el recorrido tour; ~ **en autobús** bus tour; ~ **turístico** sightseeing tour

recto straight

el recuerdo souvenir

el regalo gift

la región region

el registro check-in (hotel); ~ **del coche** vehicle registration

la regla period (menstrual)

el Reino Unido United Kingdom (U.K.)

la relación relationship

rellenar v fill out (form)

el reloj watch; **~ de pared** wall clock

el remolque trailer

reparar v fix (repair)

el repelente de insectos insect repellent

repetir v repeat

la resaca hangover

la reserva reservation; **~ natural** nature preserve

reservar v reserve

el/la residente de la UE EU resident

respirar v breathe

el restaurante restaurant

retirar v withdraw; **~ fondos** withdrawal (bank)

retrasarse v delay

la reunión meeting

revelar v develop (film)

revisar v check (on something)

la revista magazine

el riñón kidney (body part)

el río river

robado stolen

robar v steal

el robo theft

la rodilla knee

rojo red

romántico romantic

romper v break

la ropa clothing; **~ interior** underwear

rosa pink

roto broken

el rugby rugby

la rueda tire (tyre BE); **~ pinchada** flat tire (tyre BE)

las ruinas ruins

la ruta route; **~ de senderismo** walking route

S

la sábana sheet

el sacacorchos corkscrew

el saco de dormir sleeping bag

la sala room; **~ de conciertos** concert hall; **~ de espera** waiting room; **~ de reuniones** meeting room

la salida check-out (hotel)

la salida n exit; **~ de urgencia** emergency exit

las salidas departures (airport)

salir v exit, leave

el salón room; **~ de congresos** convention hall; **~ de juegos recreativos** arcade; **~ de manicura** nail salon

¡Salud! Cheers!

la salud health

las sandalias sandals

sangrar v bleed

la sangre blood

el santuario shrine

la sartén frying pan

la sauna sauna

el secador de pelo hair dryer

la secreción discharge (bodily fluid)

la seda silk

sediento thirsty

la seguridad security

el seguro insurance

seguro safe (protected)

el sello n stamp (postage)

el semáforo traffic light

la semana week

semanal weekly

el seminario seminar

el sendero trail; **~ para bicicletas** bike route

el seno breast

sentarse v sit

separado separated (marriage)

ser v be

serio serious

el servicio restroom (toilet BE); **~** service (in a restaurant); **~ completo** full-service; **~ de habitaciones** room service; **~ inalámbrico a internet** wireless internet service; **~ de internet** internet service; **~ de lavandería** laundry

service; **~ de limpieza de habitaciones** housekeeping service

la servilleta napkin

sí yes

el sida AIDS

la silla chair; **~ para niños** child seat; **~ de ruedas** wheelchair

el símbolo symbol (keyboard)

sin without; **~ alcohol** non-alcoholic; **~ grasa** fat free; **~ receta** over the counter (medication)

la sinagoga synagogue

el sitio de interés attraction (place)

el sobre envelope

el socorrista lifeguard

el sol sun

solamente only

soleado sunny

solo alone

soltero single (marriage)

el sombrero hat

la somnolencia drowsiness

sordo deaf

soso bland

el suavizante conditioner

el subtítulo subtitle

sucio dirty

la sudadera sweatshirt

el suelo floor

el sujetador bra

súper super (fuel)

superior upper
el supermercado grocery store, supermarket
la supervisión supervision
el sur south
el surfista windsurfer

T

la tabla board; ~ **de snowboard** snowboard; ~ **de surf** surfboard
la talla size; ~ **grande** plus size; ~ **pequeña** petite size
el taller garage (repair)
el talón de equipaje luggage [baggage BE] ticket
el tampón tampon
la taquilla locker; ~ reservation desk
tarde late (time)
la tarde afternoon
la tarjeta card; ~ **de cajero automático** ATM card; ~ **de crédito** credit card; ~ **de débito** debit card; ~ **de embarque** boarding pass; ~ **internacional de estudiante** international student card; ~ **de memoria** memory card; ~ **de negocios** business card; ~ **postal** postcard; ~ **de seguro** insurance card; ~ **de socio** membership card; ~ **telefónica** phone card
la tasa fee
el taxi taxi
la taza cup; ~ **medidora** measuring cup
el teatro theater; ~ **de la ópera** opera house
la tela impermeable groundcloth [groundsheet BE]
el teleférico cable car
el teléfono telephone; ~ **móvil** cell [mobile BE] phone; ~ **público** pay phone
la telesilla chair lift
el telesquí ski/drag lift
la televisión TV
el templo temple (religious)
temprano early
el tenedor fork
tener v have; ~ **dolor** v hurt (have pain); ~ **náuseas** v be nauseous
el tenis tennis
la tensión arterial blood pressure
la terminal terminal (airport)
terminar v end
la terracotta terracotta
terrible terrible
el texto n text (message)
el tiempo time; ~ **weather**
la tienda store; ~ **de alimentos naturales** health food store; ~ **de antigüedades** antique store; ~ **de bebidas alcohólicas** liquor store [off-licence BE]; ~ **de campaña** tent; ~ **de deportes** sporting goods store; ~ **de fotografía** camera store; ~ **de juguetes** toy store; ~ **de música** music store; ~ **de recuerdos** souvenir store; ~ **de regalos** gift shop; ~ **de ropa** clothing store
las tijeras scissors
la tintorería dry cleaner
el tipo de cambio exchange rate
tirar v pull (door sign)
la tirita bandage
la toalla towel
la toallita baby wipe
el tobillo ankle
el torneo de golf golf tournament
la torre tower
la tos n cough
toser v cough
el total total (amount)
trabajar v work
tradicional traditional
traducir v translate
traer v bring
tragar v swallow
el traje suit
tranquilo quiet
el tren train; ~ **rápido** express train
triste sad
la trona highchair
el trozo piece
la tumbona deck chair
el turista tourist

U

último last
la universidad university
uno one
la uña nail; ~ **del dedo** fingernail; ~ **del pie** toenail
urgente urgent
usar v use

V

las vacaciones vacation [holiday BE]
vaciar v empty
la vacuna vaccination
la vagina vagina
la validez valid
valioso valuable
el valle valley
el valor value
el vaquero denim
los vaqueros jeans
el vaso glass (drinking)
el váter químico chemical toilet
vegetariano vegetarian
la vejiga bladder
vender v sell
el veneno poison

venir v come
la ventana window
el ventilador fan (appliance)
ver v see
verde green
el vestido dress (piece of clothing)
el viaje trip
el vidrio glass (material)

viejo old
la viña vineyard
la violación n rape
violar v rape
el visado visa (passport document)
visitar v visit
la vitamina vitamin
la vitrina display case
viudo widowed
vivir v live

vomitar v vomit
el vuelo flight; ~ **internacional** international flight; ~ **nacional** domestic flight

Z

la zapatería shoe store
las zapatillas slip-pers; ~ **de deporte** sneaker
los zapatos shoes
la zona area; ~ **de compras** shopping area; ~ **de fumadores** smoking area; ~ **para picnic** picnic area
el zoológico zoo
zurcir v mend

INDEX

Berlitz pocket guide

LANZAROTE
& FUERTEVENTURA

Fifth Edition 2018

Editor: Rachel Lawrence
Author: Pam Barrett
Head of Production: Rebeka Davies
Picture Editor: Tom Smyth
Cartography Update: Carte
Update Production: Apa Digital
Photography Credits: AWL Images 1; Chris
Coe/Apa Publications 102; Corbis 21; Harry
Laub/imageBROKER/REX/Shutterstock 22;
iStock 4MC, 4ML, 6L, 99, 101; Mary Evans
Picture Library 17; Neil Buchan-Grant/Apa
Publications 4TC, 4TL, 5T, 5TC, 5MC, 5M,
5MC, 5M, 6R, 7, 7R, 11, 13, 14, 18, 24, 26, 29,
31, 32, 35, 36, 37, 39, 41, 43, 44, 47, 48, 49,
50, 51, 53, 57, 59, 61, 62, 63, 65, 66, 69, 71,
72, 73, 74, 75, 77, 79, 80, 83, 85, 86, 88, 91,
92, 94, 97, 104; Shutterstock 28, 33, 55
Cover Picture: iStock

Distribution
UK, Ireland and Europe: Apa Publications
(UK) Ltd; sales@insightguides.com
United States and Canada: Ingram
Publisher Services; ips@ingramcontent.com
Australia and New Zealand: Woodslane;
info@woodslane.com.au
Southeast Asia: Apa Publications (SN) Pte;
singaporeoffice@insightguides.com
Worldwide: Apa Publications (UK) Ltd;
sales@insightguides.com

Special Sales, Content Licensing and CoPublishing
Insight Guides can be purchased in bulk
quantities at discounted prices. We can
create special editions, personalised jackets
and corporate imprints tailored to your
needs. sales@insightguides.com;
www.insightguides.biz

Contact us
Every effort has been made to provide
accurate information in this publication,
but changes are inevitable. The publisher
cannot be responsible for any resulting loss,
inconvenience or injury. We would appreciate
it if readers would call our attention to any
errors or outdated information. We also
welcome your suggestions; please contact
us at: berlitz@apaguide.co.uk
www.insightguides.com/berlitz